Matching Hatches Made Easy

10 Steps to Catch More Trout

Charles Meck

HEADWATER BOOKS

STACKPOLE BOOKS

0 11557 00797 8

To my wonderful wife of 53-plus years,
Shirley W. Meck

Copyright © 2012 by Stackpole Books

Published by
STACKPOLE BOOKS
5067 Ritter Road
Mechanicsburg, PA 17055
www.stackpolebooks.com

Printed in the United States

First edition

Illustrations by Dave Hall
Cover design by Caroline Stover
Cover photo by Jay Nichols

10 9 8 7 6 5 4 3 2 1

Library of Congress Cataloging-in-Publication Data
Meck, Charles R.
    Matching hatches made easy : 10 steps to catch more trout / Charles Meck.
        p. cm.
    Includes index.
    ISBN-13: 978-0-8117-0797-8 (pbk.)
    ISBN-10: 0-8117-0797-0 (pbk.)
    1. Flies, Artificial. 2. Trout fishing. 3. Fly tying. 4. Aquatic insects. I. Title.

SH451.M4365 2012
688.79124—dc23
                                                                    2011038757

Contents

Acknowledgments

C atching and fishing a Brown Drake hatch in preparation for this book was no small task. Phil Baldacchino of Kettle Creek Outfitters kept me posted on the progress of the hatch on north central Pennsylvania's Kettle Creek. Chris Kenney and Bob Foresti aided me tremendously in photographing the Brown Drake on Skaneateles Lake just southwest of Syracuse, New York.

Thanks also to Kevin Mead for setting up a trip to Oregon and the Western March Brown on the McKenzie River.

On May 6, 2010, my wife Shirley went to Heaven. For more years than I would like to remember she battled arthritis, heart disease, stroke, back and hip problems, and much more. More than I could ever endure. The grandchildren called her the warrior. In spite of constant pain she was friendly, helpful, and kind. She was my greatest fan and continuously promoted my books. The first thing she'd say to anyone she had just met was "Do you know how many books he wrote?" She would then list them all. She never said I was fishing too much—although I was.

Her two devoted children and their spouses, Lynne Nowaczek and her husband Rick and Bryan Meck and his wife Julie, and I will miss her sorely and we will remember and love her every day of the rest of our lives.

Her grandchild Lauren Nowaczek wrote this tribute to Shirley at her funeral on behalf of Matthew Nowaczek and Pierce Meck:

> This is just a little note from Lauren, Matt, and Pierce because we love you more than anything. We want you to know you will always be in our heart and that we will always love you no matter what. We want you to know that you will never be forgotten and that you are one of the best grandmas a grandkid could ever ask for. We know you're in a better place now but we do wish you were here with us. We love you gaga and we always will. You will always be in our hearts and minds whenever we make decisions in life and if we ever need someone to talk to we will shout up to you, so you

be sure and listen for us! We love you and always will. You will never leave our hearts. Since the day we were born you were caring, loving, and worrying about us. You have always put everyone else before you, which truly makes you a wonderful person. Happy Mother's Day Grandma, you were and are one of the greatest grandmother/mothers ever. We will always miss you and your smiles.

That says it all.

Introduction

I've had the benefit of fishing the hatches for more than 50 years, and times have changed quickly and dramatically. I can remember days when hatches, outstanding highly productive hatches like the Sulphur, appeared and you'd have an entire section of the stream to yourself. That same section today during a Sulphur hatch might hold 25 anglers within feet of each other casting at rising trout. It reminds me of opening day all over again, but this time it's midseason. Hatches bring unbelievable crowds. Great, dependable, spectacular hatches produce the worst. Crowded waters require new tactics.

A hatch occurs when insects appear in the water column and on the water's surface in heavy enough numbers to encourage fish to feed. My primary goal in this book is to distill all I have learned about the hatches into an easy-to-read guide that will help you catch more fish.

I've learned quite a bit from my fly-fishing errors of the past. Fifty years ago I'd carry just a few patterns that matched the hatches. Now I carry patterns for all the major hatches. But I carry more for those hatches that I never saw or never thought I'd see. Flies like Color Matcher and Quick Trim flies are new. Yes, I know that in fly fishing, especially fly patterns, nothing is new, but I assure you've probably never seen these patterns before—and they catch trout. And they will help you avoid those situations when you have no match for what is hatching.

Another book on the hatches by Charlie Meck?! you might say to yourself. That makes nine books he's written about the subject. Why so many? Why are hatches so important? Can he say anything new about them?

My primary goal in this book is to distill all I have learned about the hatches into an easy-to-read guide that will help you understand and identify trout-stream insects—without a degree in entomology—and catch more fish by doing so.

If you have not yet encountered a downright spectacular hatch, this book should help. Once you've found the hatch, I include an all-new easy-to-use hatch key for some of the more common mayflies, stoneflies, and caddisflies, to give you, I hope, some ideas for matching the hatch and catching increasingly tough-to-catch trout.

WHAT IS A HATCH?

Trout feed on many forms of food. Prevalent among those are mayflies, stoneflies, and caddisflies. In his classic book, *Trout Streams*, Paul Needham found that these three make up 60 to 90 percent of a trout's diet. He also found that other insects such as midges and terrestrials make up an important part of the diet.

A hatch occurs when enough insects appear in the water column and on the water's surface to encourage fish to feed. Even landborne critters like cicadas, grasshoppers, ants, and moths can create hatchlike situations. Fish feeding on the surface are not only a wonderful sight, they are easier targets than fish that are feeding under the water.

Some hatches bring a stream alive. I have had streams that looked like they didn't have a trout in them start to boil with feeding fish during a hatch. But more has to happen than just the hatch to have rising trout. A hatch can occur and the water can be too cold for trout to feed, or trout feed only on the nymphs and emergers and not on the duns. Hatches can make that trip one you'd like to and probably will forget or one that will remain a vivid recollection for years. If you encounter a spectacular hatch—and you have the right match—you can come away from the experience with a lifetime of memories.

Many of the best hatches that I've encountered were great because the insects couldn't take flight quickly and lingered on the surface. Anything delaying the hatch that appears on the surface is a boon to the dry-fly fisher. In addition to hatches—adults emerging from nymphs (mayflies and stoneflies) or pupae (caddisflies and midges)—insects can come back to the water after mating to either die or lay eggs. These occurrences also create great feeding opportunities and I discuss them in the book.

A hatch can change the way you fish forever. I never forced my son, Bryan, to fly-fish. By the time he was 12 he was an accomplished spinner fisherman. I'll never forget that day when his whole philosophy on fishing and fishing lures changed dramatically, and within an hour. It happened on the Bald Eagle Creek in central Pennsylvania on a late May afternoon with a sporadic hatch of March Browns on the water. Bryan used one of his

Bryan Meck holds a rainbow trout from a recent spring trip to the McKenzie River in Oregon. We timed our trip to hit the famous Western March Brown hatch.

favorite Mepps' spinners and I matched the hatch with a size 12 March Brown dry fly. These large March Brown naturals brought plenty of trout to the surface and my fly was the perfect match. Now Bryan was very competitive even at that early age, and the more trout I caught the more frustrated he became. Bryan cast to every trout that rose in his vicinity, but to no avail. Trout completely refused his spinner while just about every one took my fly. That one incident forever changed the way Bryan fished for trout. On the way home that evening he vowed to use only flies for trout. He has lived up to that promise.

THE 10 SIMPLE STEPS

In this book, I will outline 10 simple steps that I have found extremely helpful in my many years of chasing hatches. In the order that they appear in the book, they are:

1. Learn bug basics.
2. Know the major hatches.
3. Fish at the right time and place.
4. Match shape and profile.
5. Be creative and unorthodox.
6. Rig multiple flies.
7. Use unconventional flies.
8. Observe nature.
9. Seek dependable hatches.
10. Pick your stream wisely.

One thing that I think you will find especially useful is my attempt at a practical key that helps you identify mayflies, stoneflies, and caddisflies. Does the mayfly have two or three tails? That's an easy way to separate many of the hatches. The key is simple and uncomplicated for all of us. The key also uses the approximate emergence date. Does the hatch appear early, middle, or late in the season? If the hatch has more than one generation or if it overlaps two of the seasons, then it's listed in both. Another characteristic I examine is the size of the insect. Is it small (size 18 hook or smaller) or is it large (16 and larger)? Coloration is also part of the key. Is the general coloration of the insect's body light or dark? Again, if an insect is a medium shade, I include it in both categories. Time of day the hatch appears is another important part of the key. Finally, the key includes another section about other distinguishing features.

You can make matching the hatches as simple or as complicated as you like. Though many anglers like to carry lots of patterns to imitate the hatches, you really only need a handful of designs that you can adapt for different insects.

There's more to matching the hatch than using an appropriate fly: There's location, weather conditions, color, and much more. You've got to find trout that will eat the fly. Timing and location can mean the difference between a frustrating event or a momentous one. I continue to see fly fishers fish an entire summer day and quit just before dusk. They have it all wrong. They should often take a break in those late hot summer afternoons and fish the last hour or two before dusk. The best time to fish in spring is from 11 a.m. to 4 p.m. The best time from May to early June to meet the hatches is from 3 p.m. to 8 p.m.; in late summer the best time is when the spinners fall from 7 to 9 p.m.

Location is important, too. You can be on the water at the right time, but be in the wrong location to encounter the hatch. Different insects prefer different habitats. Just a couple of years ago I fished Pine Creek one late May evening. Around 7 p.m. some Coffin Flies (spinners of the Green Drake) began mating and dropping to the surface to exude their fertilized eggs. I immediately tied on a Coffin Fly but had no strikes in a 15-minute period. On one cast the spinner pattern sank a few inches beneath the surface and a trout immediately struck the sunken fly. Later that evening, after the hatch was over, I stopped in a store and started to talk about the great Coffin Fly spinnerfall I had just experienced. The three anglers said, "What hatch?" They fished a few miles downstream but never experienced that Coffin Fly spinnerfall.

Also, no matter how thoroughly you plan to fish a hatch, much often does go awry and the hatch doesn't appear or one you hadn't planned for appears. To help compensate for the wonderful element of chance, I like to carry flies that I call Color Matcher and Quick Trim flies. Color Matcher flies are totally white and tied in sizes from 10 to 20. Take a series of permanent marking pens in a variety of colors and color the fly to match the hatch. Quick Trim flies are tied in two sizes—one on a size 14 dry-fly hook that covers all sizes of insects from a 10 to a 16 and a second smaller version tied on a size 18 hook that covers hatches in sizes 18 to 22. Just trim the wing and the body of the fly and start using the right colored pen. With the Color Matchers, select the proper size for the hatch that's emerging and start coloring.

Enjoy reading this book, then try some of these new tactics and techniques; you will, I hope, find matching the hatches made much easier.

Learn Bug Basics

1

The more you know about the feeding habits of trout and the more you recognize what they are feeding on, the better angler you'll be. I recently had a friend complain to me that he conducted a stream survey in early May and found no Trico nymphs. Yet the summer before he fished over great Trico spinnerfalls in the same area of the same stream. In Robert Hall's thesis at the University of Minnesota he indicated that Tricos overwinter as eggs not nymphs, and these eggs don't hatch out until mid to late May of the next year. That information alone is a reason to know a bit

It is imperative that you know a little bit about the behaviors of the foods that trout eat. While you don't need to know the Latin name of every insect, it is helpful to understand where and when it emerges, major physical features, and the habitat it prefers, among other things.

about life cycles. The White Fly nymph appears about the same time—late May. So you would not fish a White Fly nymph or a Trico nymph early in the fishing season, since there aren't any larvae in the stream at that time.

Another example where some knowledge of a specific hatch can be a valuable asset to the fly fisher occurred on Penns Creek several years back. For several years I hit fairly heavy Slate Drake hatches in late May and early June. There's one problem—at that time of year the Sulphur, Green Drake, and March Brown mayflies also compete for the trout's attention and they often don't key in on the Slate Drakes. But the Slate Drake along with a dozen other common species appears twice a year—two generations—and the second appears in mid to late September. This September hatch, however, is smaller because the nymph has only four months to develop. I generally use a size 12 pattern for the spring and a size 14 for the fall hatch. The Slate Drake becomes important in early fall because the hatch competes with few other hatches at that time of year.

> **TIP**
>
> Male and female duns of the same species can vary tremendously in color. Or two different insects may be hatching at the same time. For these reasons, fishing two different dry flies at the same time can be effective.

I planned to search for a hatch on Penns Creek several years ago in the third week in September on a cool overcast afternoon. Drakes began appearing around late afternoon into early evening. Trout rose as if the hatch might be the last one of the year—which it is. A pattern copying that late fall hatch caught plenty of trout, and for several hours trout fed on this fly. Again, a little knowledge—the hatch appears twice a year, and the second generation is smaller—goes a long way to help the angler catch more trout.

Mayflies can create incredible feeding frenzies for trout. Sometimes when these aquatic insects appear they do so in unbelievable numbers and trout gorge themselves. But more than just mayflies can create fishable hatches. Stoneflies and caddisflies regularly spend some of their time in view of trout. Trout can feed on the nymphs or larvae of both of these orders of insects. And that's not all—terrestrials like ants can fall onto the surface and create hatchlike conditions. Who hasn't seen trout feed readily and regularly on midges, crane flies, alderflies, and other insects? Trout also feed heavily on food such as annelids (worms), crustaceans, and much more. If at all possible, fish during a hatch, but remember: you won't have good fishing during the hatch unless you have a match for that hatch.

INSECT STAGE IMPORTANCE

Mayfly Common Name	Scientific Name	Nymph	Dun	Spinner
Black Quill	Leptophlebia cupida	3	6	7
Blue Quill	Paraleptophlebia adoptiva	3	2	8
Blue-Winged Olive dun	Drunella cornuta	4	3	2
Brown Drake	Ephemera simulans	2	2	1
Green Drake	Ephemera guttulata	2	1	1
Hendrickson	Ephemerella subvaria	3	2	3
Light Cahill	Stenacron interpunctatum	4	3	6
Little Blue-Winged Olive	Baetis tricaudatus	3	2	4
March Brown	Maccaffertium vicarium	3	2	5
Quill Gordon	Epeorus pleuralis	7	2	7
Slate Drake	Isonychia bicolor	5	3	6
Sulphur	Ephemerella invaria	2	1	2
Summer Blue Quill	Paraleptophlebia guttata	5	5	8
Trico	Tricorythodes spp.	6	6	3
Yellow Drake	Ephemera varia	3	3	5

This chart rates the nymph, dun, and spinner as food sources for trout, one being the best. You'll note that some duns are more important in some species and spinners more important in others. Emergence time for the dun and the method the spinner uses in laying eggs have a lot to do with the rating.

MAYFLY LIFE CYCLE

A life cycle looks at the stages an insect (like a mayfly) goes through from beginning to end. For many mayflies (order Ephemeroptera) the entire cycle is completed in approximately one year. There are many exceptions to the yearlong cycle and some are completed in several weeks. Others last for as long as three years. A brief look at a typical life cycle of a mayfly helps the angler more readily understand how mayflies fit into the scheme of things and will help in matching a hatch with a particular pattern. The life cycle will also prepare the fly fisher to better match and time the hatches and

MAYFLY LIFE CYCLE

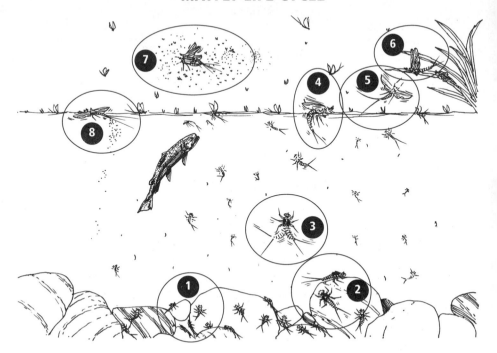

1. Most mayfly nymphs live for about one year.
2. Before emergence, nymphs become active and their wing pads darken.
3. Nymphs twist, turn, wiggle, or swim toward the surface.
4. Nymphs float helpless in the surface film as they transform from emergers into adults.
5. Newly hatched duns fly away to streamside vegetation to hide and to molt into spinners.
6. Spinners have clear, glasslike wings.
7. Males and females form a mating swarm that resembles a cloud of smoke.
8. Female spinners lay their eggs on or below the water's surface.

predict what will happen next. Life cycles help you know where, when, and how mayflies behave beneath and above the surface.

Female and male adults, called spinners by anglers, meet most often over a stream or lake. Mating while in flight, the females then lay their fertilized eggs. On moving water, male spinners often form their mating flights over stretches of fast water. On lakes and ponds, male spinners undulate directly over the shoreline and mate with females coming from nearby trees or bushes. These spinners usually have glassy, clear wings with some barring on some of the mayfly species. Some spinners dive underwater to lay eggs (*Baetis*); some fall to the surface (*Ephoron*); while others drop eggs from above the surface. The eggs laid by the female spinner incubate usually for a couple of weeks. Some female spinners like the diminutive Trico lay about 800 eggs in a dark olive ball. This ball or sac of eggs falls apart in the water. After a couple weeks, larvae or nymphs emerge from the eggs. These nymphs then inhabit various areas of the stream. Some nymphs live in weeds (some Blue-Winged Olive duns). A good number of mayflies and caddisflies live as nymphs on the undersides of rocks (March Brown and Western March Brown). Still other nymphs are free swimmers (Slate Drake) and live freely on the bottom. A dozen species (*Ephemera* species like Green, Yellow, and Brown Drakes) burrow into the substrate to live out their nymphal existence. The nymph part of the cycle lasts about 340 days, so trout have plenty of time to feed on this phase of the cycle. Some nymphs inhabit fast-water sections, others more moderate, and still others in slow water or lakes and ponds.

> **TIP**
>
> Nymphs are available to trout much longer than are duns and spinners. Mayflies live their lives as duns and spinners two to three days and as growing larvae or nymphs for more than 300 days. While matching hatches is a thrill, if you want to consistently take trout, you must imitate nymphs.

Nymphs vary tremendously in size as they grow. During its development, a nymph increases in size by splitting its exoskeleton (the hard outer covering). Each nymph can go through 10 to 20 of these changes, called instars. Remember, copying a March Brown with a nymph in September you might use a size 20 nymph. To copy that same larva in May you'd use a size 12 nymph. About a year (some emerge in less than a year and some after two or three years) after the spinner lays its eggs, the nymph transforms to a dun.

Some mayfly nymphs emerge (change to duns) near the bottom of the stream; some near the middle; and some near or on the surface. There are many bottom emergers like the Quill Gordon (*Epeorus*) and some of the Sulphurs and Blue-Winged Olives (*Ephemerella* and *Drunella*). Some species like the Gray and Slate Drakes (*Siphlonurus* and *Isonychia*), Tricos (some species), and others swim to shore or to an exposed object in the stream or lake as nymphs and then change to a dun. Other aquatic insect orders like caddisflies go through a resting stage or pupal phase before they emerge as adults. This stage can last for a week or two. Those that include all the stages (egg, nymph or larva, resting stage, and adult) have complete metamorphosis. Those missing the resting stage are said to have incomplete metamorphosis. Stoneflies and mayflies lack the resting stage or pupal stage and therefore have incomplete metamorphosis.

The process of changing from an underwater insect to an air-breathing one often takes time. This emerger stage in which the nymph transforms into a dun is one of the most vulnerable in the entire life cycle of the may-fly (the phase where the spinner falls spent on the surface is equally important—but in this stage there is less food value). Trout sense that emergers are defenseless and readily feed on them.

In a few minutes to a day or more after it emerges, the dun again changes by shedding its outer skin and becoming a mating adult or a spin-ner (also called an adult or imago by scientists) usually with glassy, clear

A throat pump sample from a Henry's Fork trout reveals its preference for Flavs.

Is Latin Important?

Knowing the Latin names for the insects can often be helpful, but it isn't necessary. In fact, trying to keep up with the Latin can overcomplicate the business of matching the hatches.

I'll never forget when I wrote extensively about the March Brown (*Stenonema vicarium*) in *Hatches Made Simple* (published in 2002). A few weeks after the book came on the market entomologists decided to change the scientific name. Scientific names are in a state of flux; common names aren't. Dozens of other scientific name changes have occurred in the past decade. The names Light Cahill and March Brown remain the same.

It's important to know what flies copy a hatch. Flies matching hatches have become important to me. But we've gone overboard in the number of patterns we use to match the hatches. Enter the Color Matcher and Quick Trim flies. I carry one simple fly in white and I carry a couple of dozen permanent marking pens to color the fly to meet the hatch. No need to carry box upon box of flies—just color the fly the correct color. On purpose on certain days I decide to use only one fly pattern and color it to match the hatches. You'll read a lot about these flies later.

wings. Male spinners are fairly easy to distinguish from females. They have longer front legs, a clasper, larger eyes, and glassy, clear wings. The dun cannot mate (except *Ephoron*). The spinner is the mating adult.

With some species like the Dark Quill Gordon (*Ameletus ludens*), members are parthenogenic and the eggs don't have to be fertilized. Therefore you will find few if any males of this species.

Male spinners of most species form a swarm over or near the water, waiting for females to join them. When the female spinners enter the swarm, the males impregnate them. The females then move toward the water's surface and deposit their fertilized eggs. Some spinners move along the surface to deposit eggs like the White Flies (*Ephoron leukon*). Spinners of other species drop eggs from a foot or two above the surface. On occasion dragging the White Fly imitation during the dun fall (the female dun never changes to a spinner) works well. Female spinners often fall to the surface spent after laying their eggs. Many spent females sink under the surface after they die.

Spinners swarm in different ways to mate. Male spinners like those of the Summer Blue Quill (Jenny Spinner) and Brown Drake Spinner (*Hexagenia atrocaudata*) characteristically rise and fall (undulate) over a stream. They fly upwards of 20 feet then drop 20 feet. The Jenny Spinner does this for 4 to 6 hours. If you see this occurring in June, July, or August, you know that this stream holds a Blue Quill hatch and that those duns will emerge around 6 or 7 a.m. Trico spinner swarms and Sulphurs act differently. The latter form loose balls of spinners and once mated do little moving. Trico female spinners enter the swarm of male spinners, mate, and move upstream. This egg-laying characteristic is the same for all spinners of a mayfly species.

> **TIP**
>
> Nymphs grow by shedding their exoskeleton. A Brown Drake nymph in October will be much smaller than one found in early May. So this means that different sizes of the same fly often work.

The length of time between the dun and spinner stages varies considerably from species to species. The White Fly and the Trico duns often change to spinners in a matter of minutes. Weather, however, can affect the change from dun to spinner. Some mayflies, especially those emerging in early spring, can take as long as two to three days to change from a dun to a spinner. Cloudy conditions, a fine drizzle, and more can delay the change from dun to spinner for days.

Eggs develop into larvae or nymphs a few weeks after fertilization. Some species like White Flies and Tricos, however, overwinter in the egg stage and transform into larvae the following spring, when water temperatures warm.

CADDISFLY LIFE CYCLE

The life cycle of mothlike caddisflies (order Trichoptera) varies considerably from that of mayflies. Most caddisfly adults sport a drab body of tan, brown, gray, or black. There are some with orange, amber, yellow, and green bodies, but more common are the dull-colored bodies. Usually caddisfly adults live for up to a month out of water—much longer than mayflies. Males and adult females meet and mate and the female then deposits her eggs. Adults deposit their eggs in many ways. Often they dive underneath and deposit them, but some deposit the eggs on overhanging branches. The eggs laid above the surface usually hatch when it rains. The eggs fall to the surface and become larvae. Female adults lay from 300 to 1,000 eggs. Females lay the eggs in gelatinous masses on sticks or other debris. The egg stage of the order Trichoptera lasts a few days and then the larvae hatch out. Most larvae build a specific type of case to protect their soft bodies. Some

CADDISFLY LIFE CYCLE

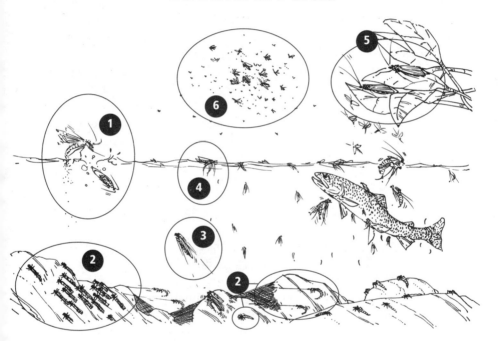

1. Female adult caddis deposit eggs on the surface of the river or dive beneath to oviposit.
2. There are three varieties of caddis larvae—case builders, net builders, and free-living. The larvae mature in about one year.
3. The larvae change into pupae. The pupal area fills with gases, helping the caddis ascend to the surface.
4. The pupae may drift for long distances before the adults break through the pupal skin.
5. Adult caddis live for several days to two weeks prior to mating.
6. Mating flights occur most often in the evening.

species are case makers, some are net spinners, while others are free swimmers (Green Caddis, *Rhyacophila*). Cases can be made from fine gravel, a piece of wood, or other plant material. For more than nine months, case makers and net spinners use the case as their home. During that time, larvae feed on other insects, plant material, and microorganisms. Before the larva emerges it enters a resting or pupal stage. This stage lasts for two to three weeks. To prepare for the pupal stage, the larva forms a cocoon and envelops itself. Free swimmers spin a silklike cocoon; whereas most case makers spin a lining inside their case.

TIP

Few male spinners fall onto the surface. If they do, then they do so very sporadically. One of the few that is important to copy is the male Trico spinner. Jenny Spinners (*Paraleptophlebia guttata*) rise and fall in the air above waters all morning long in the summer. Rarely do these spinners fall onto the surface in any numbers.

In the two to three weeks the caddis spends in the case, it develops its entire adult body, except wings. At emergence time pupae bounce along the bottom and trout readily feed on them. To help split the case when emerging, the pupa cuts its case with its strong mandibles. Adults live under bridges, on trees, and other protective places. Some adults mate in daylight, especially some of the early hatches, but most appear in the evening.

Caddisflies emerge just about any time of the year. The Grannom appears in heavy numbers in the East in mid-April and its relative in April and May in the West. Hatches continue into October with the emergence of the October caddis. I have seen huge orange-bodied caddisflies emerge in late March on the Metolius River in Oregon.

Caddisflies also present several opportunities for trout to prey on them: when as pupae they are ready to emerge, the emergence process, and the egg-laying phase. Caddisflies, like mayflies, sometimes emerge malformed and are unable to escape. Trout often feed on these cripples long after the hatch has ended.

Dave McMullen has guided anglers on Eastern waters for 30 years. He estimates that in those 30 years he has spent 24,000 hours with clients. Much of that is over the Grannom and pre-Grannom activity on Spruce Creek and the Little Juniata River in central Pennsylvania. He says that like clockwork the Grannom caddis larvae pupate around the middle of March and hatch near the middle of April every year. He has noticed that

Many species of caddis larvae live in cases made from rocks, vegetation, or other material. Trout will eat the case and all.

Caddisfly adults look like moths. Trout love feeding on egg-laying or spent adults.

Grannoms need fast water to emerge or break out of their pupal skin. If, however, they emerge in slower water, they can't break out and trout feed eagerly on these stillborn caddisflies.

STONEFLY LIFE CYCLE
The stonefly order (Plecoptera) is an ancient one. Nymphs live underwater in faster sections of clean streams and rivers. Small stoneflies often emerge in a year; larger ones in two or three years (*Pteronarcys*). Nymphs can be

STONEFLY LIFE CYCLE

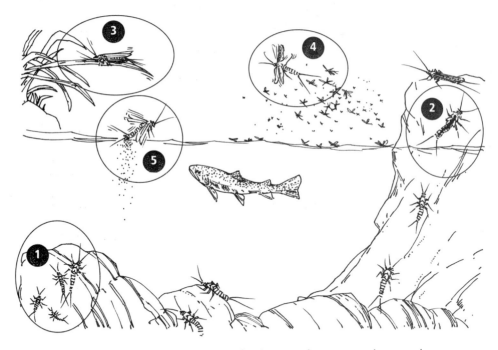

1. Eggs develop into nymphs. Some stoneflies live up to four years, so there are always several different sizes of nymphs in the stream.
2. Nymphs migrate to the water's edge and crawl out of the water onto a rock, log, or tree. They shed their exoskeletons and become adults.
3. Stoneflies mate while at rest on streamside vegetation or on the ground.
4. Clumsy adults fall in the water from nearby bushes or while in flight.
5. Females oviposit on the surface of the water.

Stonefly nymphs (Golden Stone pictured above) are common in unpolluted trout streams across the country.

omnivorous (eating plant and animal material), carnivorous (animal), or herbivorous (plant). They grow just like mayflies by breaking their exoskeletons (called instars). Some species do this more than 20 times. When they are ready to emerge as adults, the nymphs crawl out of the water onto a tree, stick, rock, or bridge abutment and molt into adults. Adults can live for a few weeks. After they mate, the females fly over the water and drop usually 500 to 1,000 eggs. Larvae hatch out in a few days.

Several stonefly species have evolved into winter emergers. Their development accelerates and adults appear on warm winter days. Members of the families Capniidae, Nemouridae, and Taeniopterygidae appear in the winter. Members of the family Capniidae, especially, emerge from December to March and give trout an important source of food when nothing else is available. I have seen some in northern Arizona on Tonto Creek crawl onto snow after they emerged.

MIDGE LIFE CYCLE

The order Diptera includes true flies. Two of the aquatic families that trout feed on are midges (family Chironomidae) and crane flies (Tipulidae). Both resemble mosquitoes.

MIDGE LIFE CYCLE

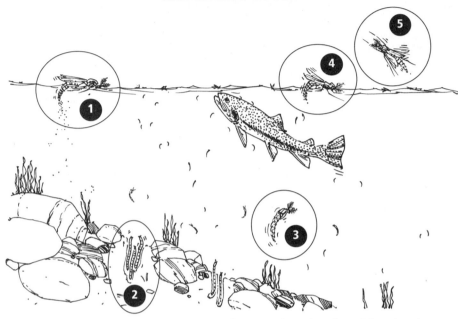

1. Female adults lay their eggs; the eggs sink into cracks and crevices of the substrate.
2. Midges have three to five broods a year. The larvae look like worms and mature in a few weeks.
3. Midges go through a complete metamorphosis, and the larvae change into pupae before becoming adults. The larva is inactive for several days, then its bulbous head fills with gases, helping it float to the surface.
4. Pupae often drift for long distances before the adults break through the pupal skin.
5. The adult flies away to streamside foliage to mate.

Midges make up an important source of food for trout. Paul Needham in *Trout Streams* said that chironomids make up the majority of food for trout under four inches long. I've, however, seen heavy trout consistently feeding on these small flies.

Midges and crane flies have complete life cycles, which include a pupal stage. Both orders pupate, emerge, and lay eggs in masses. Some larvae are free living while others live in a case made by the larvae. Midge larvae feed mainly on plant material. They can emerge in incredible numbers, usually in the evening. A size 16 to 22 Zebra Midge is one top producer almost the entire year.

OTHER INSECTS
Other orders of insects can also create notable hatches.

Ants
Members of the family Formicidae can cover trout waters of the East. On August 25, plus or minus 10 days, anglers will find thousands of ants on the surface of many of their favorite trout streams of the East. From late summer through September, trout will feed on these terrestrials for hours.

How does the lowly ant become an important food source? Ants form colonies. To form a new colony, winged males and females leave the old colony in late summer and mate in flight, similarly to mayflies. Because of their characteristic swarming flight as part of their life cycle, they move a good distance. And like the mayfly, the male winged ant dies after mating and many of these fall on the surface of streams. Females search for a suitable site to lay their eggs and a colony is formed.

Grasshoppers
The grasshopper life cycle encompasses three phases—egg, nymph, and adult. Eggs normally are laid by the adult female in late autumn. In April and May of the next year these eggs hatch out into nymphs. These nymphs feed on vegetation. Nymphs resemble adults, but have no wings and are smaller. The nymph sheds its cuticle five times (called molts) and grows to the adult stage in about 40 days.

This simple foam grasshopper pattern, called the Charlie Boy Hopper, is easy to tie, durable, floats well, and imitates grasshoppers, crickets, and even adult stoneflies or cicadas when tied in the appropriate color and size.

Wings begin appearing and become more refined after each molt. After the last molt (fifth) the wings unfold and the nymph becomes a mating adult.

The adult stage is often reached in early July to mid-August. Grasshoppers mate and egg-laying continues into September. Body colors of the adult run from yellow or green to brown. If food is scarce, grasshoppers will migrate up to 100 miles. Use smaller patterns in the spring to copy the nymph and a larger winged pattern in midsummer and autumn.

Western Spruce Moth

The spruce moth life cycle begins with eggs deposited in the tops of evergreen trees in late August. These eggs hatch out into larvae in September and the immatures immediately go into cocoonlike cases. In spring when the evergreen buds are developing, the larvae emerge from their case and feed. These worms feed for a couple of months, pupate, and then become wing-mating adult moths. Adult flying moths appear in late July and much of August. Spruce moths are clumsy fliers, and in the process of mating a wind blows them onto the surface of a trout stream. Trout eagerly feed on the adult copied by a size 10 or 12 tan Elk Hair Caddis because there are scant hatches in late summer. The larger the infestation by the spruce moths, the better the hatch matching. Look for adults to be active from late morning into early afternoon. Adult moths die near the end of August. Many rivers in Idaho, Montana, and Washington experience this unusual "hatch."

Periodical Cicadas

Nymphs of the cicada live underground up to two feet deep for 2, 13, or 17 years, depending on the species. Often called 17-year locusts, these nymphs appear aboveground and then crawl up a tree or other vegetation. Some of the species important as trout food appear aboveground once every 17 years in late May or early June.

Adults are capable of flying but are rather clumsy and often land on the water's surface. Trout go crazy over this huge morsel, and for four to six weeks the correct orange or black pattern can catch humongous trout. You know when the adults have appeared by the noise the male makes during the mating period. Fertilized females deposit eggs in the tips of trees. These tips fall to the ground, and the eggs hatch out after about six weeks. These young nymphs then crawl underground and stay there feeding on the roots of trees until its time to emerge.

VARIATION IN SIZE AND COLOR

The same species of mayfly duns and nymphs can vary in size and color. Some species vary more in color than others. The widest ranges in colors can be found in the Pale Morning Dun (*Ephemerella excrucians*). In one year of fishing this hatch in the West I found some members of this species with reddish tan abdomens, others with olive, and some with yellow bellies. This insect seems to vary more than any other species.

BODY COLOR VARIATION		
Mayfly Species	Female	Male
Baetis and related spp.	Tannish brown body	Hyaline body with last few segments darker
Epeorus vitreus dun	Pinkish cream body	Creamish yellow body
Ephemerella invaria spinner	Tan body	Brownish body
Ephemerella needhami dun	Olive-green body	Dark brown body
Ephemerella subvaria dun	Tan body	Reddish tan body
Paraleptophlebia spinner	Dark brown body	Hyaline body with last few segments dark brown
Stenacron interpunctatum dun	Pale orange body	Pale yellow body
Tricorythodes dun	Pale olive body	Dark brown body
Tricorythodes spinner	Cream body with last two or three segments dark brown	Body is totally dark brown

Body color among mayflies often varies from male to female. The best example is
Ephemerella needhami where the female is olive-green and the male is dark brown. Be
prepared with patterns that copy both sexes.

Some mayfly species vary considerably from male to female, with the
male usually darker than the female; and the female brighter than the male.
The Trico male dun is dark brown, whereas the female dun is pale olive-
cream. The male Ephemerella needhami is dark brown and the female is
bright green-olive. The female Pink Lady (Epeorus vitreus), however,
is pink-cream and the male has a pale yellow abdomen. The same goes for
the general coloration of the male and female Light Cahill (Stenacron
interpunctatum).

Mayflies also vary in color from stream to stream. On some smaller
streams, the March Brown sports a very dark brown back. On many larger
waters, the same species is lighter in color. The Green Drake also varies considerably in color and size from stream to stream.

Some mayflies also change color the longer they are exposed to the air.
Paul Weamer wrote a comprehensive guide to fishing the Delaware River, in

which he describes this phenomenon. He found that when they first appear on the surface of the Delaware River, Slate Drake duns have a distinct olive cast, which they soon lose after being exposed to the air. Paul believes that in copying the emerging dun, it's important to fish a fly with an olive coloration.

Most spinners vary in color depending on whether they have mated and laid their eggs. They can also vary in color from male to female. A Coffin Fly (*Ephemera guttulata*) female with eggs still in its body has an abdomen of creamish yellow. A female that has exuded all of its eggs and falls spent on the surface has a chalky white body.

Color Prediction

The predominant body color of mayflies in early spring is brown, dark tan, olive gray, or dark gray to black. (See the table with species having different body colors in the males and females on page 17.) Mayflies like the Blue Quill (dark gray); Quill Gordon (tannish gray); Dark Quill Gordon (*Ameletus ludens*, dark slate gray); Hendrickson (tan); Red Quill (reddish brown); Western March Brown (tan and brown); and the Black Quill (slate gray) emerge early in the fishing season. Look at the down-wings that appear at the same time. They exhibit the same colors in early spring. The Grannom caddis has a dark gray to black body, the Little Black Caddis a black body, and the Early Brown Stonefly has a dark brown body. So if you're fishing a stream or river for the first time in early spring, you'd probably select a dark gray, brown, or dark-tan-bodied fly. If you want to fish a down-wing pattern, then try one with a black, dark gray, or brown body.

In the summer months, more brightly colored mayflies, stoneflies, and caddisflies appear and colors like white, tan, cream-yellow, and yellow-olive are the dominant colors of the evening hatches. (Of course there's an exception to every rule, including this one. Pale Morning Duns in the West normally emerge in daylight hours.) At that time you have the Sulphur (olive-yellow), Light Cahill (yellow), White Fly (white), Green Drake (cream), Yellow Drake (yellow), and more. Green and tan caddisflies usually appear in May.

Grays and olives like the Blue-winged Olive Dun and Blue Quill still appear in the summer, but they most often do so in the morning and afternoon. There are a few spectacular hatches like Slate Drakes (gray), Brown Drakes (yellowish brown), and Hex (tannish brown) that appear on summer evenings. But, bright-colored mayflies appear in the evening.

In the fall months, the colors usually include grays and olives. Hatches like the Slate Drake, Blue Quill, or Mahogany Dun (gray) and Little Blue-Winged Olive dun (olive-gray) appear. Why this change in color pattern from season to season? Protective coloration! Tracy Storer in *General Biology* says that protective coloration keeps many species (including aquatic insects) in harmony with their surroundings. That is, they blend in with the colors of nature. The predominant colors of nature in early spring and winter are tans and grays.

Look at the rocks along a stream, or the gray leafless branches of a tree—all drab gray or tan colors. Doesn't it make sense that these vulnerable hatches mimic the colors of their environment? Colorful mayflies appear most often when color, in the form of leaves and flowers, fills the environment. Note that there are no mayflies appearing early in the season that have light backs. Why? When mayfly duns emerge from the water, they most often rest for a day or more

> **TIP**
>
> If you are unfamiliar with the water and the hatches that appear, you can carry several Color Matcher or Quick Trim flies. For spring carry permanent marking pens with colors of tan, brown, gray, and olive; for summer take browns, grays, yellows, creams, and pink pens; and for fall carry gray and olive pens. A knowledge of the colors that are prominent in aquatic insects limits the number of pens you have to carry with you. If you are uncertain of the size of the flies, then carry Quick Trim flies.

before they come back to the stream to mate and lay eggs. Where do they rest for that day or two? You'll most often find them on rocks near the stream (especially if the weather is cold) or on branches of a nearby bush or tree. Normally mayflies rest on the underside of leaves. But leaves have not yet appeared for the season. What predominant color will you find in the rocks near the shore and bushes and branches? The only colors are tan, brown, and dark gray. Over the eons, mayflies that did emerge with lighter-colored backs were easy fodder for predators like birds. Those mayflies with darker backs were less easy to see and they prevailed.

How does this information affect a fly fisher's choice of patterns in the early season? After learning the general seasonal coloration of mayflies would you select a Light Cahill or a Dark Cahill to match most of the April hatches? Of course you'd select the darker pattern.

Second, look also at the hatches for midseason. Just about all hatches that appear during the day are dark in color. This is nature's way of protecting them. This doesn't mean that all dark mayflies appear during the day, but those that do are usually dark. Mayflies that commonly appear on summer mornings are Blue Quills (gray) and Blue-Winged Olives (olive).

How is this color phenomenon useful to the angler? It limits the number of choices you have to make, especially if you are fishing strange waters. If you want to copy what trout have been eating on a summer evening and there is no hatch at the present time, then try a Light Cahill. Fish an Adams or Blue-Winged Olive dun to match the grays and olives of summer and fall mornings. Try a tan Hendrickson or a gray Quill Gordon in the spring— even if there currently is no hatch. A general knowledge of what colors appear when can help you minimize the pattern selection dilemma dramatically, especially if you plan to fish unfamiliar waters.

> **TIP**
>
> Some nymphs live on rocks (*Stenonema*); others live in vegetation (*Ephemerella*); other nymphs are free swimming (*Isonychia*); and larger nymphs often burrow in the bottom of the stream (*Ephemera* and *Hexagenia*). Know also where in the stream the dun emerges— midstream, on rocks, or the edge of the stream. Knowledge of where the nymph changes to a dun can help you fish more appropriately. Slate Drakes often climb onto a rock to emerge. Gray Drakes often climb out of the water and onto submerged vegetation to emerge. You might want to fish nymphs of these species differently than those that emerge in the stream.

Size

Mayflies, caddisflies, and stoneflies also vary in size. First, they vary in size from stream to stream; second, they vary in size from male to female; third, they vary in size from one generation to another. In addition, if you're fishing a nymph, that nymph size varies from initial larva to emergence time.

Let's look at the final statement first. Nymphs vary in size from the time they first hatch from an egg into a larva until they emerge as a dun. For example, when the Sulphur and PMD emerge in late May (later in high Western rivers) anglers match the emerging dun with a size 16 dun or nymph pattern. But what happens in July, August, and September if you want to copy the same insect? In August you might copy the Sulphur nymph that will hatch the next May with a size 22 nymphal pattern. The following April you might want to use a size 18 wet fly. In order to grow, nymphs shed their outer skin, called the exoskeleton, many times. These events are called instars and this is how the nymph grows.

Nymphs and their emerging duns vary in size dramatically from stream to stream. In some of the larger mayflies, the size variation is much more noticeable. Anglers accurately copy the Green Drake on central Pennsylvania's Penns Creek with a size 8 dun. If they fish the same hatch on Cedar Run, 50 miles to the northeast, anglers more accurately copy that hatch with a size 10 pattern. Why the difference in size? In two words: food supply.

Many aquatic insects also vary in size from male to female. Often the male is smaller than the female, as in some mayflies like Light Cahills, Yellow Drakes, and many others.

Nymphs and duns also vary in size from one generation to the next. Look at the Slate Drake as an example. Slate Drakes hatch in late May and a second generation appears in mid-September. The September generation has only three and a half months to mature, but the May generation matures in eight and a half months. Slate Drakes in late spring are matched with a size 12, those in fall with a size 14.

Is size important? Size and profile are two of the most important particulars when matching a hatch. If you want to match a hatch and experience a successful outcome, then you've got to remember this and copy the size correctly. And it is best to carry several sizes of the same pattern.

Size and color of nymphs, duns, and spinners of the same species can vary from stream to stream, from male to female, and from one generation to another. Males are often a size smaller than the female and often a bit darker than the female.

But variation in size and color is not limited to mayflies. The huge Salmonfly stonefly varies considerably in size—and color. It and other large stoneflies take two or three years to mature. With such a long life cycle, some stoneflies naturally encounter a better food supply than others. Size can also vary for caddisflies. Look at the Grannom in the East and the Mother's Day hatch in the West. Some of these critters can be copied with a size 16 down-wing while others are better copied with a size 14 fly.

HABITAT

Habitat, or where the nymph lives and emerges into an adult, is important to the fly fisher. I can remember some fly fishers complaining because they fished a slow pool on a top limestone stream in the peak of the hatch and saw very few Sulphur duns. While the hatch still appeared, I took them downstream a few hundred yards to more variable water. There the Sulphur hatch was in full swing and at least a dozen trout fed. By moving a couple hundred yards, they hit a hatch. The emergence chart in chapter 6 (page 84) devotes a column to habitat where you'll most often find the nymph—in fast, medium, or slow water. Follow the habitat listings carefully if you want to hit the peak of the hatch.

WHEN HATCHES APPEAR

From Edmunds' *The Mayflies of North and Central America*, I first became aware of V. Landa's article, "Developmental Cycles of Central European Ephemeroptera," which discussed emergence times of mayflies. First and most common are those that appear once a year and have one generation. He divided mayflies that appear once a year into three categories, however: One in which eggs hatch in fall and the nymphs continue to grow; an example of this is the Slate Drake (*Isonychia bicolor*). In the second, eggs are in diapause until spring. Two examples of this are the White Fly (*Ephoron leukon*) and the Trico (*Tricorythodes* in northern zones). And in the third, nymphs hibernate over winter; some *Ephemerella* like the Sulphur follow this path.

The next group of mayflies are those produce two or more generations per year. This group is further divided into four categories. In the first twice-a-year category the first generation eggs hatch in fall, the nymphs develop throughout the winter, and the second generation appears during the spring or summer. An example of this is the Little Blue-Winged Olive (*Baetis tricaudatus*). The Little Blue-Winged Olive appears in March and April and again in September and October. In the second category the eggs go into diapause in the winter, then two more generations appear in the summer. The Trico in its northern climes is an example. In the third category first generation eggs hatch in fall, adults emerge in spring, and two generations appear in the summer. *Callibaetis* species (or Speckle-Winged Duns) are representatives of this group. Finally, in the fourth twice-a-year category some eggs hatch in the fall while others of the same species hatch in spring; adults emerge as two separate broods in the summer. Some *Baetis* exhibit this type of emergence.

Landa's third group of mayflies takes two or three years to develop into adults. The Green Drake (*Ephemera guttulata*) is an example of the two-year phase and the Hex (*Hexagenia limbata*) is an example of a three-year cycle.

Many insect hatches are heaviest during rotten weather. Note the dark, ominous skies in the background.

The fourth and last group has two generations in three years or three generations in two years. *Baetis tricaudatus* is an example of the latter type.

Although Landa's divisions are helpful, weather also affects the hatching capability. Look at the Trico on the Salt and Verde rivers in Arizona. Trico spinners appeared in the air on the Salt River, 15 miles from Phoenix, on New Year's morning. Hatches also appear in November. The heaviest hatch I've ever seen was the hatch on the Verde River, 70 miles north of Phoenix, on February 15. In the northern part of the United States the Trico has two generations (bivoltene); in some northern areas of Canada the Trico has just one generation (univoltene).

What about insects other than mayflies? Most caddisflies require a year to complete their life cycle. There are a few, some with a portable case, that have several broods a year and others that take more than a year to complete their life cycle. All of these variables affect the emergence date of the hatch.

We know that some large stoneflies take two or three years to complete their life cycle. The giant Pteronarcys of the West, the Salmonfly, has a three year emergence. Cicadas appear every 2, 13, or 17 years depending on the species. McCafferty in his epic book, *Aquatic Entomology*, reports that some arctic midges require 5 to 7 years to complete one generation. He also reports that some members of the order Diptera require just a week to complete a generation. Those that require the least amount of time will appear most of the fishing season.

Spruce moths, which appear annually in late July and August, can be compared with the Gypsy Moth (appears a month or two earlier in the East). Both have one generation each year.

TIME OF DAY

You can almost set your watch by the time that some species emerge or spinners fall. Look at the Blue-Winged Olive dun (*Drunella cornuta*) that appears in late May. On many fertile waters the hatch continues to emerge until early July. The hatch most often appears around 11 a.m. The adult of this species, the Dark Olive spinner, mates and falls around 7 p.m. The first couple of days the Sulphur (*Ephemerella invaria*) hatch appears—usually the second week in May—hatches often appear in the afternoon. But as the hatch progresses it appears at 8:30 p.m. Many times anglers just sit and wait or rather stand and wait for any action. Seldom much happens before 8:30. The Yellow Drake also presents another great example. Look for this hatch on slow sections of streams in mid to late June at 8:45 p.m. I venture to guess that more than half of an evening's Yellow Drake duns appear within 15 minutes of that time.

> **TIP**
>
> Use gray flies like an Adams in the spring and fall and a light-colored pattern like the Light Cahill on summer evenings.

Of course times the hatches appear vary with temperature and weather. Hendrickson hatches can appear as early as 9:00 a.m. on hot April days and as late as 6:00 p.m. on others. On several occasions, Phil Baldacchino of Kettle Creek Tackle Shop reports that Brown Drakes on unusually warm days appear in the morning. Pale Morning Duns in the West hatch in the morning, afternoon, and evening. On the Kootenai River, one of the heaviest Pale Morning Dun hatches that I've ever seen appeared continuously from late morning until early evening.

Trico spinners fall early morning in the heat of July and August and later as fall approaches. I've seen Trico spinners fall in October and November well past noon. How can this help you? Plan your trip earlier in mid-summer and later in the fall to hit the Trico spinnerfall.

A s I was ready to leave Hoagland Branch one late July evening, I checked a spider web on a bridge crossing the small, secluded mountain stream. I was dumbfounded when I saw several small mayfly spinners still alive in the web. When I examined them closer I found that they were Tricos. That very evening I had to head to another location to fish the next morning. But finding this Trico upset the entire schedule. I postponed that 100-mile trip so I could see a Trico hatch on this small, heavily canopied mountain stream the next morning. Tricos emerge and

Tricos, above, along with Blue-Winged Olives and Sulphurs/PMDs, represent one of the big three hatches found across the United States. If you fish in the morning during the summer, make sure you have Trico spinner imitations in your box.

mate in the morning for about three months, so I knew I'd see the hatch the next morning.

That next day I arrived at the stream at 7 a.m. in anticipation of the hatch. I had never witnessed one on a freestone stream this small and one so heavily tree-lined. I didn't have to wait long. Shortly after I arrived Tricos began emerging and in a while spinners gathered over the fast water just upstream from me. Within a few more minutes two trout fed on fallen spinners. This small stream didn't hold a spectacular hatch; however I did catch trout. Had I not identified the hatch in that spider web and known when the hatch appears, I would have missed it.

Why is it important to know which hatch is appearing? First, if you know the hatch, then you will probably use the correct pattern. Second, if you know the hatch, you're probably familiar with any unusual characteristics the hatch might display. Finally, if you know the hatch, you'll know which phases are important and when the spinner appears. If you know the hatch, you'll recognize how trout react to the hatch. For example, even when the huge Green Drake emerges, trout often feed on a smaller mayfly, the Sulphur, that appears at the same time. If you recognize this, then you are prepared for frustrating circumstances. In his classic book, *Caddisflies,* Gary LaFontaine wrote: "The important advantage a fly fisherman gains with that knowledge is the ability to predict trout feeding patterns—and consequently to suit his techniques to those patterns."

Because mayflies and caddisflies are the largest group of hatching insects, I will focus on them. Stoneflies and midges are also important, but most members behave the same, so you don't need to key them down to species.

MAYFLY ID MADE EASY

The more you know about the hatches, the better prepared you'll be to fish them. But how in the world, especially if you are just starting to learn to fly-fish, do you get to know the hatches? The identification key in this book will help you tremendously (see page 169). It's nonscientific and easy to use. The key is based on several distinguishable characteristics of mayflies: time of year, number of tails, overall size, and overall coloration. If you know these four variables, then you can identify many of the hatches. If insects are on the border between light and dark, or large and small, then they are listed in both categories.

NUMBER OF TAILS					
Mayfly family	**Scientific Name**	**Time**	**Common Name**	**Nymph**	**Dun**
Ameletidae	*Ameletus ludens*	E	Dark Quill Gordon	3	2
Baetidae	*Baetis tricaudatus*	M, A, E	Little Blue-Winged Olive	2	2
	B. intercalaris	M, A, E	Little Blue-Winged Olive	2	2
	Callibaetis skokianus	E, M	Speckle-Winged Dun	2	2
	C. ferrugineus	E, M	Speckle-Winged Dun	2	2
	Diphetor hageni	M	Dark Brown Dun	2	2
	Plauditus veteris	A	Little Blue-Winged Olive	2	2
Caenidae	*Caenis hilaris*	M	Little White Mayfly	3	3
	Tricorythodes spp. (several)	M, A	Trico	3	3
Ephemerellidae	*Attenella attenuata*	M	Blue-Winged Olive	3	3
	Dannella simplex	M	Blue-Winged Olive	3	3
	Drunella cornuta	M	Blue-Winged Olive Dun	3	3
	D. flavilinea	M	Blue-Winged Olive Dun	3	3
	D. grandis grandis	M	Western Green Drake	3	3
	D. grandis ingens	M	Western Green Drake	3	3
	D. lata	M	Blue-Winged Olive Dun	3	3

Number of tails is a very important identifying characteristic for mayflies. This chart lists the number of tails for the nymph and dun of many mayfly species. Note that in some cases, the nymph has more tails than the dun.

NUMBER OF TAILS continued

Mayfly family	Scientific Name	Time	Common Name	Nymph	Dun
Ephemerellidae	D. walkeri	M	Blue-Winged Olive	3	3
	Ephemerella dorothea dorothea	M	Pale Evening Dun	3	3
	E. dorothea infrequens	M	Pale Morning Dun	3	3
	E. invaria	M	Sulphur	3	3
	E. needhami	M	Male: Chocolate Dun; Female: Olive Sulphur	3	3
	E. subvaria	E	Male: Red Quill; Female: Hendrickson	3	3
	Eurylophella bicolor	M	Chocolate Dun	3	3
	Penelomax septentrionalis	M	Pale Evening Dun	3	3
	Teloganopsis deficiens	M	Dark Blue Quill	3	3
Ephemeridae	Ephemera guttulata	M	Green Drake	3	3
	E. simulans	M	Brown Drake	3	3
	E. varia	M	Yellow Drake	3	2
	Hexagenia atrocaudata	M	Big Slate Drake	3	2
	H. limbata	M	Michigan Caddis	3	2
	H. rigida	M	Green Drake	3	2
	Litobrancha recurvata	M	Dark Green Drake	3	2
Heptageniidae	Cinygma dimicki	M	Light Cahill	3	2
	Cinygmula ramaleyi	M	Pale Brown Dun	3	2
	Epeorus albertae	M	Pink Lady	3	2
	E. longimanus	E	Quill Gordon	3	2
	E. pleuralis	E	Quill Gordon	3	2

NUMBER OF TAILS continued

Mayfly family	Scientific Name	Time	Common Name	Nymph	Dun
Heptageniidae	E. vitreus	M	Male: Light Cahill; Female: Pink Cahill	3	2
	Heptagenia elegantula	M	Pale Evening Dun	3	2
	H. marginalis	M	Light Cahill	3	2
	H. pulla	M	Pale Evening Dun	3	2
	H. solitaria	M, L	Gray Fox	3	2
	Leucrocuta aphrodite	M	Pale Evening Dun	3	2
	L. hebe	M	Pale Evening Dun	3	2
	Maccaffertium ithaca	M	Light Cahill	3	2
	M. modestum	M	Cream Cahill	3	2
	Rhithrogena futilis	M	Quill Gordon	3	2
	R. hageni	M	Pale Brown Dun	3	2
	R. morrisoni	E	Western March Brown	3	2
	R. undulata	M	Quill Gordon	3	2
	Stenacron interpunctatum	M	Light Cahill	3	2
Isonychiidae	Isonychia bicolor	M, L	Slate Drake	3	2
Leptohyphidae	Tricorythodes allectus	M, L	Little Olive Dun; Trico spinner	3	3
	T. fictus	M, L	Little Olive Dun; Trico spinner	3	3
	T. stygiatus	M, L	Little Olive Dun; Trico spinner	3	3
Leptophlebiidae	Leptophlebia cupida	E	Black Quill	3	3
	L. johnsoni McDunnough	M	Iron Blue Quill	3	3
	Paraleptophlebia adoptiva	E	Blue Quill	3	3
	P. debilis	M	Blue Quill	3	3

	NUMBER OF TAILS continued					
Mayfly family	Scientific Name	Time	Common Name	Nymph	Dun
Leptophlebiidae	P. guttata	M, L	Blue Quill	3	3
	P. memorialis	E	Blue Quill or Mahogany Dun	3	3
	P. mollis	M	Blue Quill	2	3
	P. praepedita	M, L	Blue Quill	3	3
	P. strigula	M, L	Blue Quill	3	3
Metretopodidae	Siphloplecton basale	E	Dark Olive Dun	3	2
Polymitarcyidae	Ephoron album	M, L	White Fly	3	2 (male), 3 (female)*
	E. leukon	M, L	White Fly	3	2 (male), 3 (female)*
	Anthopotamus distinctus	M	Golden Drake	3	3
Siphlonuridae	Siphlonurus alternatus	M	Gray Drake	3	2
	S. quebecensis	M	Gray Drake	3	2

*Females don't change to spinners.

Number of Tails

Counting the number of tails is simple and will help you narrow the possibilities quickly. Some have two, others have three, and in a few species, like the White Fly (*Ephoron*), males have two tails and females three. If the middle tail is only half the length of the other two tails, then the hatch might be the Black Quill (*Leptophlebia cupida*).

Some nymphs of a species have three tails and the dun and spinner have only two. But no two-tailed nymph develops into a three-tailed adult. Tails are extremely fragile; make certain when examining mayflies that none of the tails is broken.

Genera with Two Tails

Baetis	*Epeorus*	*Litobrancha*
Callibaetis	*Ephoron* (male)	*Pseudocloeon*
Cinygma	*Heptagenia*	*Siphlonurus*
Cinygmula	*Hexagenia*	*Stenacron*
Cloeon	*Isonychia*	*Stenonema*

Genera with Three Tails:

Anthopotamus	*Drunella*	*Leptophlebia*
Attenella	*Ephemerella*	*Serratella*
Caenis Ephemera	*Ephoron* (female)	*Paraleptophlebia*
Dannella	*Eurylophella*	*Tricorythodes*

The Season

In the key on page 27, the time of year the hatch appears is divided into early, middle, and late. Early includes hatches appearing from January 1 to April 30. Middle covers those mayflies appearing from May 1 to August 31, and late includes insects emerging from September 1 to December 31. Of course there are plenty of exceptions. Hatches do appear in late fall, winter, and very early spring. In warmer locations of the Southwest, Trico spinner-falls occur in January and February. Fish the McKenzie River in Oregon just south of Portland on a late February afternoon and you'll probably see trout rising to a Western March Brown hatch *(Rhithrogena morrisoni).* You might also find on that same Western river an occasional October caddis and giant Salmonfly appear in late March or April—months ahead of the suggested emergence time. And don't forget, many species produce more than one generation each year. If any species habitually appears in two of the periods, they are listed in both.

Emergence dates of some of the major spring hatches are earlier now than they were 50 years ago. Call it global warming or what you will, April hatches are now appearing earlier than they did a half-century ago. In 1977 in *Meeting and Fishing the Hatches* I listed the Henricksons' emergence as April 26, and now their emergence date is at least six days earlier.

Hatches appear as much as four to six weeks earlier or later than the dates listed in the hatch chart on page 84, depending on weather and location. Generally,

Three-tailed nymphs produce two- or three-tailed adults. This *Ephemerella* nymph has three tails in the nymph, dun, and spinner stages.

hatches appear earlier than the date listed south of central Pennsylvania and later north of that area. The farther you travel in each direction, the more the date varies.

Mayflies usually appear at the most comfortable time of the day. In early and mid-April that means you'll see most of the hatches in early afternoon from 1 to 3 p.m. As the season progresses and air temperatures warm, many hatches revert to the cooler morning and evening hours to emerge.

Tailwaters, cool springs, and extremely cold waters delay hatch dates. Green Drakes appear on Penns Creek in central Pennsylvania near the end of May. Fish just downstream from where Elk Creek enters and you can find Green Drakes there a week later. Jonas Price at the Feathered Hook in Coburn first alerted me to this phenomenon on Penns Creek. The Frying Pan River and the Western Green Drake hatch is the same. The Green Drake begins at Glenwood Springs around June 25 on the Roaring Fork. The hatch moves upstream daily a mile or so ending up at the bottom-release, Ruedi Reservoir, around the beginning of September.

> **TIP**
>
> Some mayflies emerge more than once a year, and this increases the likelihood that you'll encounter them. Slate Drakes emerge in late May and early June and a second generation appears in mid-September. Little Blue-Winged Olive duns (*Baetis tricaudatus*) also produce two generations each year.

General Coloration

A third identifying feature is the color of the insect. Determining whether the bug is light or dark can be subjective. Look at the March Brown as an example. Examine the top or back of this large mayfly and you see a dark brown insect. Look at the underside of the March Brown and you see a pale cream belly ribbed finely with dark brown. That same coloration scheme goes for many other aquatic insects.

Gray and olive insects tend to appear in the spring and fall and during the daylight hours in the summer. Cream insects generally appear in late spring and summer evenings. How can you use this information? Of course, you can use gray flies like an Adams in the spring and fall and a light-colored pattern like the Light Cahill on summer evenings. If bright yellow mayflies appeared before flowers bloomed and trees leaved, they'd have no place to hide. That is the premise for my book *The Hatches Made Simple*.

Trico hatches can provide exciting fishing on streams across the country—at a time when little else is hatching—but they are not always dependable.

Early-Season Colors
Morning and afternoon:
   Tans, browns, dark grays, and grays

Midseason Colors
Morning and afternoon:
   Olive and gray
Evening:
   Light-colored mayflies: white, cream, yellow, and olive-yellow
   Dark-colored mayflies: gray, brown, and yellow-brown

Late-Season Colors
Afternoon:
   Gray and olive

When I prepared the manuscript for *Meeting and Fishing the Hatches* back in 1977 I sent Wills Flowers, a skilled entomologist, male spinners from several Rocky Mountain streams for him to identify. I remember sending him mayfly spinner males with a reddish brown body, an olive one, and a cream one. The identification for all three came back as the same species—the Pale Morning Dun (*Ephemerella excrucians*). Wills told me that this species, possibly more than any other, varies in color from stream to stream, and it varies in color even on the same stream.

I wrote earlier that males and females of the same species can vary tremendously in color. *Ephemerella needhami* is a great example of this phenomenon. The female dun has a greenish olive body and the male dun a dark brown one. The Trico spinner is another example. The male is dark brown, almost black, and the female almost white with some brown markings.

Size of the Insect

Size, large or small in the key, is again subjective. Generally the larger mayflies are those tied on a size 16 or larger hook—most of the large mayfly patterns are tied on hooks from 6 to 16. Those listed as smaller are usually copied with pattern sizes 18 to 26. A word of caution: The same insect can vary in size from stream to stream. Anglers copy the Green Drake on Penns Creek with a size 8 fly. They match the same hatch on Cedar Run, 50 miles to the northeast, with a size 10 or 12 fly.

Other Features

To further help you identify some of the mayflies, I've added comments that might set one mayfly off from another, like if male and female duns have different colors. Many of the features in this column refer to coloration of the mayfly. The hatch chart on page 84 lists most of the common mayflies and the number of tails the dun, spinner, and nymph possess. Examples of some of the other features that help you identify the hatch are items like timing of the hatch, color of the abdomen, number of generations each year, differences in body coloration between the sexes, number of generations each year, and length of tails. If the male is smaller than the female this feature is mentioned.

CADDIS ID MADE EASY
Number of Tails

As with mayflies the most positive, scientific way of identifying a caddisfly is studying the genitalia. But the chart will help. Why isn't the number of tails listed in the identification chart for down-wings? All stoneflies possess two tails, caddisflies have no tails.

Early, Middle, and Late Hatches
Most caddisflies and stoneflies have a one-year life cycle and most appear the same time each year. The Grannom of the East and the Mother's Day hatches of the West are very specific in the time of their appearance. And both are extremely widespread and tremendously important to match. The Grannom most often appears the third week in April and its close relative in the West near the second week in May. Most down-wings are as predictable as mayflies. How do you think the October Caddis of the West got its name? There are, however, exceptions. Many of the larger stoneflies have two- and three-year life cycles. The *Pteronarcys* of the West, the Salmonfly, and the close relative of the East, the Giant Stonefly, take three years to mature. The more time spent as a nymph, the more room there is for variation in hatching time. Also some caddisflies have more than one generation per year.

> **TIP**
>
> Knowledge of the insects' requirements will help you find them. For instance, a heavy canopy affects some mating flights. Trico spinners with their characteristic movement need plenty of room to form the mating swarm, so the best swarms occur in open, sunny areas.

The time of year that the hatch appears is important. The Animas River in southern Colorado holds plenty of spectacular caddisfly hatches. Many of these, however, appear in the middle of runoff in May and June and therefore are not readily fishable. Farther north runoff continues often into July, so fishing the hatches is chancy even into mid-July.

General Coloration
Most down-wings are dark on their dorsal (back) and ventral (belly) side. But there are lighter colors. The Light Stonefly has a yellow abdomen, the Yellow Sally a bright yellow one, and the Little Green Stonefly a bright green one. Many of the hatches of the West in midsummer, however, are either dark brown, dark gray, or black.

Variation in Color
Anglers name most caddisfly hatches by the color of the natural's belly. Green Caddis have green bellies, Yellow Caddis have—you guessed it—yellow bellies. But down-wings can vary in color. I have seen the Salmonfly on different waters with abdomens from pale to bright orange. The Little

Green Stonefly found on northeastern Pennsylvania's Mehoopany is a brighter green color than the same species found on other nearby streams.

Size of the Insect

The Delaware River in the East holds a generous supply of Giant Stoneflies. To the West a hundred miles, the same species appears on Smays Run. At both places the hatch takes three years to complete its life cycle, but the *Pteronarcys* of the Delaware has a much better food supply than Smays Run. The Smays Run adult stonefly is smaller than the same hatch on the Delaware. The same goes for other stoneflies and many caddisflies like the Grannom. Size can vary depending on the food supply of the down-wing.

Adult Salmonflies (above) and Golden Stones provide a significant meal for trout, though size can vary. When fishing over selective or pressured trout, try fishing an imitation one size smaller than the naturals.

Time of Day

Like mayflies, many caddisflies and some stoneflies appear at the most comfortable time of day. Little Black Caddisflies, Light Stoneflies, Grannom caddisflies, Early Brown Stoneflies, Spotted Sedges, and others appear in April and May. Many of these same down-wing species appear during the daylight hours. If you fish the Kootenai of northwestern Montana in late July during the day, you'll probably encounter little if any insect activity. But fish a fast-water section around 8 p.m. and you'll see thousands of Dark Gray Caddisflies in the air and on the water with plenty of rising trout. In June, July, and August the Kootenai, Ruby, Clark Fork, and the Bighorn of the West come alive with caddisfly hatches in the evening.

Other Features

Other features can be helpful in identifying down-wings: the coloration of the adult, the size of the adult, and when it appears. These features, along with emergence characteristics, can help you in identifying the hatch.

Fish at the Right Time and Place

Timing can make or break a fishing trip! Many anglers aren't able to plan their trips around a particular day or time. How many can just take a day off in the middle of the week when a hatch appears? But you can follow a series of rules to plan for meeting the hatches.

For years I took a week's vacation in mid-April to fish the Loyalsock Creek in north central Pennsylvania. Invariably I hit one or all of the following hatches: Blue Quill, Hendrickson, or Quill Gordon. To be at the right place at the right time you need more than a day or two.

Throughout this chapter I have included some of my most telling hatch stories, case studies if you will, that have all taught me important lessons about meeting and fishing the hatches.

Kettle Creek Outfitters in north-central Pennsylvania displays patterns to copy the hatches. The list changes weekly during the fishing season.

CASE STUDY 1 **Bitterroot River, Western Montana June 25, 1978**

I arrived on the stream on June 25 one hour earlier than the usual 11 a.m. emergence time of the dark olive Green Drake, tied on a large Western Green Drake imitation, and sat back and anxiously waited—no, hoped—for the hatch to appear. I had no previous knowledge that the hatch would appear, but if it did, the date I waited on the river, June 25, and the time, 11 a.m., were appropriate. In about half an hour the first large dark olive-black mayfly appeared on the surface, struggled to free itself from its nymphal shuck, and disappeared into the mouth of a large Bitterroot cutthroat. The same fate happened to the next natural that rested too long on the surface. Two insects on the surface and two trout captured them. It was time to cast my imitation. I made that first cast above a third riser to a Green Drake natural and it smashed that artificial like it was the real thing.

Wow! The very first cast on a Western river and an 18-inch cutthroat on the end of the line. The sporadic hatch lasted for more than an hour and my imitation duped a half dozen large trout.

In the time since taking my inaugural fishing trip West more than 30 years ago (read case study #1, above), I developed a method for fishing the hatches—a series of rules that I still follow today when I want to fish the hatches. Some of these rules were first listed in *Meeting and Fishing the Hatches* (1977), and they are still as important as ever. In the ensuing years I have added a few more to help you meet and successfully fish the hatches.

RULE 1. Choose a probable date the common species emerges.
Select a common hatch that emerges for two, three, or four weeks. For instance, the Sulphur first appears on central Pennsylvania's Little Juniata River around May 8. It continues to appear every evening for the next three weeks, well into June. If you want to fish that hatch on that river, select a date like May 16 and be on the stream at 7 p.m., an hour or more ahead of the hatch. If you hit inclement weather, plan to arrive even earlier.

The Western Green Drake on Colorado's Frying Pan River is also predictable. This gargantuan insect first emerges on the Roaring Fork at Glenwood Springs around June 25 and continues upriver and then up a tributary—the Frying Pan—ending at the Ruedi Reservoir around September 1. The hatch moves upriver a mile or two each day. Once you know where the hatch is, you can readily predict where it will be. Fishing the hatch is another story since much of the Frying Pan River is now posted against trespassing.

In the Green Drake hatch I hit on the Bitterroot River, I had no previous knowledge whether that river held the hatch or not. It was an educated guess to fish that river at that time. But the mayfly did appear at the time I expected, and I had plenty of effective imitations. Remember, you've got to adjust your emergence dates based on the location. Western Green Drakes appear on the Metolius River in central Oregon around May 25 and on or about June 25 farther inland on waters like the Henry's Fork in Idaho and the Bitterroot River.

Craig Josephson fishes Reservation Creek in northern Arizona. Several streams as far south as northern Arizona hold Western Green Drake hatches.

CASE STUDY 2

West Branch Delaware River, Balls Eddy area, Pennsylvania, 11:30 a.m., April 15, 2010

Dan Raymond has been fishing the hatches for more than 50 years. He lives in two locations, Connecticut and the Pocono Mountains in Pennsylvania. When he commutes, which is often, he crosses one of the top rivers in the East, the Delaware River. He and one of his fly-fishing companions, Paul Canebari, planned a trip to the Delaware River in 2010. They wanted to fish a Hendrickson hatch, so they planned well ahead of time for that event. First, they decided to look and fish for the hatch on the Pennsylvania side of the upper Delaware River. This river holds possibly the greatest hatch of Hendricksons of any water in the United States. The hatch normally appears in the early afternoon, so the two anglers arrived at 11:30 a.m. Once the hatch begins, you can expect it to continue daily on the river for more than a week. The day they selected to look for the hatch was April 15. This date is a good two weeks early for the hatch on the Delaware, but spring 2010 was not normal. In late March, much of the East experienced temperatures in the high 80s and low 90s for several days. Hatches all over the Northeast appeared early. Anglers missed many hatches because they occurred before the official fishing season opened. Paul had checked with several local anglers who frequent the river and they told him that the hatch had

If you wonder whether a hatch has begun or not, check with some locals who fish the water frequently or a local fly shop. These fly shops can be a wealth of information on what's hatching. In fact, I've seen a number of the better shops post the hatches presently appearing on local streams and rivers on a chalkboard outside the shops. Here then are some suggestions to help you find out if the hatch is on—and where to fish it.

- Network with locals on the stream.
- Check with local fly shops.
- Hire a guide (see page 50).
- Check forums on the Internet.

started a couple of days ago. So he and Dan felt confident they'd hit that specific mayfly.

No sooner had the two anglers arrived on the river than they began to see swirls and dimpling on and just under the surface. Dan assumed they were rising to emergers, so he tied on a pattern to copy that phase of the Hendrickson. He picked up four trout quickly in the riffle and then looked downriver and saw another pod of trout rising there. It was 12:15 p.m. by the time he waded downriver a hundred feet where he saw 15 to 20 trout feeding freely in front of him. He picked up a few more heavy trout in this new location on the same emerger pattern. By 1 p.m. Hendricksons began emerging by the hundreds, and the mouths of large trout actually came out of the water grabbing laggard duns and emergers trying to escape. In the next half, hour Dan released five more trout 14 to 20 inches long. And it didn't take long-distance casting to reach them—most of those trout rose within 30 feet of Dan. Then Dan saw a good fish taking a combination of duns and emergers in front of him and he adequately covered the riser. Within seconds a huge mouth opened up, grabbed his emerger, went deep, and Dan set the hook and this huge monster jumped out of the water several times. Thirty minutes later, Paul Canebari skillfully netted the behemoth for Dan in his small catch-and-release landing net, which only held half of the fish. The brown trout measured 28½ inches long. Yes, that's not a typo.

RULE 2. Plan to fish at the proper time and place for a specific hatch.
Many hatches like the Western March Brown, Hendrickson, and Western Green Drake are highly time specific. Prepare ahead for the hatch and appear on the stream ahead of the emergence time. And always remember: Most mayflies emerge at the most comfortable time of the day. That means many hatches appear in the morning and afternoon in the spring and evening in the summer. In the fall many of the hatches appear in late afternoon. The Western March Brown most often appears from 1 to 3 p.m. The Western Green Drake usually begins its daily appearance around 11 a.m. I arrived at 10 a.m. and the hatch didn't appear for almost an hour for that inaugural Western Green Drake hatch. Had I no previous knowledge that the drake

South Island, New Zealand
February 1988

Mike Manfredo and I spent the entire month of February 1988 on New Zealand's South Island. We fished that spectacular island for 29 solid days. After all that fishing I still have questions in my mind about the angling on the South Island. First, where are all the small trout? In that entire month we caught very few trout under 12 inches long. Second, what the devil do those trout feed on? Only on two occasions did we encounter honest-to-goodness hatches. A spectacular hatch appeared on the Waikaka River near Gore and an early morning spinnerfall on the Oreti River near Lumsden.

Now most anglers when they go to New Zealand hire a guide—but we didn't. We were frugal to a fault. And that one error cost us dearly for the first week we fished. We were foreigners to this country and all we had to rely on was a series of magazine articles about the streams and rivers of the South Island.

Because of the paucity of hatches, just about all we did was sight fishing. A guide usually spots the fish for you and you do the rest. We didn't have that advantage. One of us would search for big trout; then the other would fish for them. I still remember vividly how that first week turned out to be a disaster. On some days that first week we were entirely shut out—no trout for an entire day of fishing. Then we decided not to follow all the stream recommendations that other authors had suggested but to go out on our own. We did better—much better. One day we asked a rancher if we could fish his stretch of the Waikaka running through his land and he said: "Only if you have dinner with us when you're finished." Can you imagine anywhere else in the world the owner inviting you to dinner after you were a guest fishing his water? I have always said that the greatest resource New Zealand has is its people.

We arrived on the stream about 6 p.m. and to our amazement we saw trout rising—plenty of them. More than a dozen trout fed in the riffle and pool in front of us. And these just weren't your normal trout; they were monsters. Now we had to figure out what these trout were feeding on. That was fairly easy—a small mayfly flew right past me and I captured it. It looked like a pattern the natives called Dad's Favourite on a size 16 or 18 hook. The natural had brown legs and tail, a gray body, and slate wings. I tied on a size 16 Blue Quill and began casting to one of the risers near me. But catching that fish was easier said or written about than done. As soon as I got within casting range, the trout took off—they scattered. I fished over the next riser and the same thing happened again—these fish were really spooky. What to do next? I stayed 50 feet from the stream's edge and crawled in a prone position until I got within about 10 feet of the stream. Then I cast from that prone position—yes, I cast in a prone position. On the first cast that I covered, the feeding trout hit and I had to stand up to fight him. That scattered the other feeding fish, but I finally landed a heavy brown.

Mike and I left the stream and sat back off the edge about 50 feet, and those panicky trout soon began to feed again. We did this four or five times until the hatch had ended. Now the water was completely quiet and we had to search for trout. What an evening of fly fishing. Here we were in a foreign land with spectacular scenery, a terrific hatch, rising trout, and a totally successful evening. As we headed back to thank the rancher, Mike and I reminisced about the great fishing brought on suddenly by an unexpected hatch. That dinner at the rancher's house ended a perfect day of fishing.

The very next morning we crossed the Oreti River near Lumsden on our way to breakfast, and we saw a half dozen trout breaking the surface for food. Mike pulled the car over quickly; we threw on our gear and finished putting the rods together as we raced toward the stream and the rising trout.

We instantly saw a spinner similar to a dark Quill Gordon, about a size 12, on the water in heavy numbers and huge trout—many over 18 inches long—fed throughout the riffle. These trout didn't seem quite as spooky as the one on the Waikaka the night before, maybe because these trout fed in a heavy riffle, and Mike and I landed a half dozen before the spinnerfall had ended. As soon as the last dead spinner floated past me, the water grew silent. Where were the trout? We quit fishing and headed for breakfast. In those almost 30 days of fishing in kiwi land, those two were the only two hatches of the month.

appears in the late morning and early afternoon and looked for the hatch at
4 p.m. I would have missed the hatch completely. Normally you wouldn't
look for an Eastern Green or Brown Drake in the middle of the morning—
but rather you'd look for them to appear around 8:30 p.m. Hendricksons
appear on the surface from 2 to 4 p.m.; Quill Gordons from 1 to 2 p.m. Of
course weather can alter these hatch times tremendously. The hatch chart on
page 84 shows approximate times the hatches appear on the surface.

The specific place or location you fish on a stream when a hatch
appears can be critical to your success.

**RULE 3. Select a common and fishable species of mayflies, stoneflies, or
caddisflies when preparing to fish the hatches.**
A common hatch is one that is found throughout an area in good numbers.
A fishable hatch is another story. It means that there are a good number of
insects appearing on the surface and slow in their escape, so that trout have

Fishing from a boat allows you to cover a lot of water and row into a better casting
position; however, it does make timing a localized hatch a little more difficult.

plenty of time to take the laggard duns or feed on the emerger nymph or spinner. In case study #2, the Western Green Drake is an extremely common hatch throughout the Western states, and many of the duns rest for several seconds before takeoff. Dan Raymond and Paul Canebari choose a very common and fishable mayfly, the Hendrickson. Other dependable hatches include the Western March Brown, Trico, Sulphur, and Pale Morning Dun. These hatches all have several things in common. First, they are prolific and emerge for a good number of days each year. On many near coastal waters of the West, the Western March Brown appears in March, April, and early May. The Trico appears for almost 90 days. In the Southwest, the Trico appears every morning for more than 150 days.

> **TIP**
>
> Many mayfly hatches move upstream daily. In the East, the Green Drake moves a couple of miles each evening on Penns Creek in central Pennsylvania. On the Roaring Fork in central Colorado, the Western Green Drake emerges in the same manner. It begins appearing near Glenwood Springs around June 25 and ends its emergence just below Ruedi Reservoir on the Frying Pan River around Labor Day.

RULE 4. Look for the hatch on a good stream, river, or lake and a good location on that water.

Dan and Paul in case study #2 on page 40 chose the Delaware River to fish the Hendrickson. Streams don't get much better than the Delaware. For the Western March Brown, Bryan Meck and I chose the McKenzie River in Oregon. In chapter 10, you'll find a list of hatches and some of the better streams and rivers that hold these hatches. If you've fly-fished long enough, you already have a good idea where some of the most productive waters are in your area. Some streams are well noted for certain hatches. The Au Sable in Michigan is noted for the Hex hatch each year; Henry's Fork in Idaho is known for dozens of spectacular hatches, among them the Pale Morning Dun; Spring Creek in central Pennsylvania for the Sulphur; and the list goes on and on. Above all—keep records of times, days, locations, and hatches that you've experienced so you can meet and fish them again and again.

Remember that one part of a stream can host a great hatch, and at other locations on that same water, the same hatch can be sporadic at best. If the hatch isn't heavy or is nonexistent where you're fishing, move. Look at chapter 10 for some locations for specific hatches.

McKenzie River, Springfield, Oregon
April 1, 2011

I fished from my first drift boat in 1984 in the McKenzie River in Oregon. That first hatch on the McKenzie occurred in mid-April with the famous Western March Brown. Our guide at that time was Ken Helfrich and he drifted us through many, many pods of trout rising to the Western March Brown in the early afternoon. He also was the first guide to show me how to fish the tandem. So guides will not only show you hatches and how to match them, but also techniques required on the river you're fishing. But best of all if you're fishing from a drift boat, you can reach just about every riser.

Twenty-seven years later I wanted to meet and fish that same March Brown hatch on the McKenzie River. The March Brown appears in the afternoon from late February into late April and early May. This time Matt Ramsey floated my son, Bryan, and me downriver 11 miles on April 1. No, this was no April Fool's joke. I mean we really experienced a great matching-the-hatch episode.

In the West, the March Brown is readily predictable. I hadn't seen the hatch for more than 20 years and I wanted photos of the natural. I contacted Kevin Mead of Lake Oswego, Oregon, and he scheduled us to fish the McKenzie on April 1. We scheduled that float trip almost a year ahead of time. Compound that with persistent rain in the Northwest, and you might begin to wonder if the hatch would appear. I seriously questioned if we should float the river that first day of April since the area had experienced rain for 28 of the past 30 days and the river was extremely high, although not muddy. After discussing our chances of seeing a hatch and rising trout, Matt decided we should take the extended float downriver. Above all I wanted to see—and capture and photograph—some Western March Browns that day. And I wanted dearly to catch trout rising to the hatch. I carried with me a butterfly net and several storage cups for any insects I collected. I waited and watched for the hatch to begin; Bryan fished as we covered the first two or three miles of the river.

We didn't drift very far before Bryan caught his first rainbow in that high water. It was a modest fish—15 inches long and a fighter. What did I do? I sat back, took photos, and waited. I waited for that elusive March Brown hatch to appear. I wanted to fish that hatch more than anything. But I had to wait. It was only 11 a.m. and the hatch was still a couple of hours from its normal appearance time. Meanwhile, Bryan caught a half dozen heavy rainbows while I sat and waited.

We went ashore at noon and had a short lunch break—still no March Browns. Bryan did grab one large stonefly. I looked at the belly of this huge down-wing and immediately identified it as a Salmonfly. Was it a cruel April Fool's joke? What was this huge stonefly doing appearing this early in the season? Adding to the huge stonefly Bryan caught a giant (33 mm) orange caddis (locals call it the Silver Striped Sedge) that appeared. Why these huge down-wings appeared in early April is still a mystery to me.

In a few minutes a heavy swarm of caddisflies appeared that looked like the Grannom of the East or the Mother's Day hatch of the West. No matter what they were, trout in this high water ate them eagerly the entire afternoon.

About 1:30 the first March Brown appeared and Matt pointed it out. Soon a few more appeared and the trout began feeding. Bryan swiped the net at two airborne March Browns and put then in a holding cup for me to take photos later. Now it was my turn to fish. Matt handed me a fly rod with a March Brown already attached and I began casting to two or three risers. Within seconds the first trout hit the March Brown and I missed it. A cast or two later and another rainbow hit the imitation. As we drifted for the next two or three miles we saw more than two dozen trout rise to March Browns and we stopped and made productive casts over many of these fish. The hatch ended by 2:30, but trout continued to rise to down-wings for a good hour after the mayfly hatch ended. What a great day matching hatches in this high water!

RULE 5. Be well prepared with a variety of patterns to copy the hatch.
No hatch is any better than the match you have for that hatch. I wasn't prepared one evening for a spectacular Brown Drake hatch and spinnerfall because of my lack of a satisfactory match for that mayfly. Carry at least one backup pattern. That second pattern should also match the hatch. I carried two different Western Green Drake flies on that trip to the Bitterroot River. That backup pattern was a fast-water variety with dark gray deer hair wings. Dan Raymond carried with him plenty of Red Quills to match the male dun, Hendricksons for the female dun, and Hendrickson emerger patterns. Carry a few Color Matcher and Quick Trim flies for those unexpected situations.

RULE 6. Some hatches last only a short time, so be prepared to change flies quickly if the first imitation doesn't work.
Hatches like the Quill Gordon, Hendrickson, and Blue-Winged Olive last for a couple of hours or less, so you don't have much time to match the hatch. During these short duration hatches, you've got to make decisions quickly. Decisions like should I move to a new location, should I change flies, and more, have to be made in minutes.

I've been known to carry two fly rods with me to the stream—both fully equipped right down to the fly tied on the tippet. If the first fly doesn't catch trout, I quickly cast that other fly rod with a second fly. When Blue-Winged Olive duns emerge in good weather, the hatch can last for less than an hour, and if you aren't prepared, the hatch can be over before you're completely ready for it.

In case study #2 on page 40, Dan stayed with the emerger throughout the hatch because that pattern caught plenty of trout through the entire hatch.

RULE 7. Be prepared for other hatches.
What happens if the hatch you plan to fish doesn't appear? Maybe warmer- or colder-than-normal temperatures have hastened or delayed the hatch. What if another hatch appears in heavy numbers—other than the one you planned to meet and fish? Be prepared for many of the secondary hatches you might see. On that trip to the Bitterroot, I carried plenty of Pale Morning Dun patterns—and that hatch did appear along with the Green Drake, but was not nearly as spectacular as the drake. I carry a compartmented fly box with me every time I fly-fish. It contains patterns for all the hatches I

It often pays to have two rods rigged up with different options, perhaps a dry-fly rig and a nymph rig, or two different dry flies. This way, you do not waste time rigging if you need to present different flies to the fish.

expect to see at that time of year. One of the compartments in that fly box is totally devoted to the hatches. I have one early, one middle, and one late match-the-hatch box that I carry with me depending on the time of year I fly-fish.

On many occasions, especially early in the season, I've seen two and even three different hatches appearing simultaneously. One day on Fishing Creek in central Pennsylvania, I hit a Grannom hatch in the morning, followed shortly by a Quill Gordon and Blue Quill, and a Hendrickson hatch appeared an hour later. Trout rose to all four hatches.

RULE 8. Fish the proper type of water.
What does this mean? The Western Green Drake lives in moderate stretches of water. You wouldn't wait for the hatch in very slow or extremely fast water. Sulphurs live in all types of water. (See the hatch chart on page 84.) I have a group of angling friends who consistently fish a slow-water stretch of a limestone stream in central Pennsylvania. Although the stretch holds plenty of trout, the hatches on this section are sparse. Anglers continue to complain that few trout rise to the hatches in this water. But move downstream where there is more irregular water—fast, moderate, and slow

Being in the right place at the right time is critical. I can't think of how many times parking lot conversations at the end of the night revealed that some anglers hit the hatch and others did not. By knowing what habitat the insects prefer, you can increase your odds of seeing a hatch.

stretches—and you'll find fairly heavy hatches and plenty of rising trout. Why does this anomaly occur? That lower section has more varied flows, and many hatches prefer faster water. You can be on the right stream at the right time for the hatch and miss the hatch by not fishing the right kind of water.

I vividly remember coming back to a lodge after an evening fishing trip to the Box Canyon area of the Henry's Fork in Idaho complaining that I saw few Brown Drakes on the water. I talked with other angling guests that evening who boasted about the great hatch they fished over and the number of trout feeding on those insects. They fished in a slow-water section just a few miles below me and had a great evening while I had a very frustrating one.

THE BENEFITS OF HIRING A GUIDE
For years I didn't hire a guide or drift boat. When I arrived in New Zealand with Mike Manfredo (see case study #4 on page 46), it took the two of us an entire week—and more—to learn the intricacies of kiwi fly fishing: search and cast. We had a month to fish, so we weren't pressed for time. It took a

| CASE STUDY 5 | Spring Creek, Central Pennsylvania
October 15, 2010, 3 p.m. |
| --- | --- |

Around 2 p.m. a few Little Blue-Winged Olives emerged, and I decided to walk upstream and see if I could find some trout feeding on the sparse fall hatch. I approached a deep pool with a bridge above, stopped, and scanned the surface for a few minutes. There, in that deep hole, under that bridge, hundreds of Little Blue-Wings emerged and trout responded by taking some of the last surface food of fall. As I left the pool, duns were still emerging and trout still rising. On my walk downstream to the car I saw only a couple of Blue-Winged Olives emerge. That bridge pool was the place to be for this particular hatch. Had I not traveled upstream to that pool I would have said that there was little or no hatch.

For October 15 it was raw and bitterly cold. The temperature never rose above 36 degrees and by 1 p.m. no hatch appeared. I moved downstream half a mile to another pool and immediately noted thousands of Little Blue-Winged Olives emerging within a foot or two of the near shore. Duns continued to appear for more than an hour and trout now fed. Before the hatch ended, I moved to other often-productive locations and never saw one dun emerge. Had I stayed at the first or the last few locations, I would not have witnessed the heavy hatch I experienced at the second location.

If you don't see a hatch and you think there should be one—move. Move upstream or downstream until you are convinced that no hatch will appear that day. Often a good indicator that a hatch is in progress is the number of cars at parking lots near the stream. Always remember: Any hatch can appear on one specific location on a stream and not on others.

week to acquaint ourselves to South Island fishing before we were successful. That is a good lesson to remember. If you only have a short time to fish—hire a guide. If you're unfamiliar with the water and you don't have much time—hire a guide. If you want to witness a hatch on a local stream—hire a guide. It'll probably be a lot more memorable trip.

Especially if you are new to a river or an area of a river I recommend strongly that you hire a local expert—a guide. Guides know more about local conditions, local techniques that work, and of course they know what, when, and where the hatches will appear. Depend on them; they can really help you! Nick Nicklas of West Yellowstone showed me the Salmonfly hatch and an appropriate pattern, the Simple Salmon, to adequately copy the *Pteronarcys* on the Madison and Firehole rivers. George Cook, a guide on the eastern lakes in Washington State, showed several of us how to fish the desert lakes of the eastern part of that state. Ken Helfrich and Matt Ramsey had me fish over Western March Brown hatches on the McKenzie River in Oregon. Dave Blackburn showed me a great PMD hatch on the Kootenai in Montana.

Guides can not only keep you posted when and where the hatches will appear; but also with their great drift boats, they can get you to rising trout easily. The older you get, the more relaxing fishing the hatches from a drift boat can be (see case study #4, page 46). Without a guide and a drift boat on the McKenzie, I probably wouldn't have been able to reach one of those rising trout. How could I have reached these risers in this near flood-stage water?

You can find guides for almost every floatable trout river of the West. That wasn't the case a few decades ago. When I worked on *Meeting and Fishing the Hatches* in 1976, I tried to hire a guide to help me fish the Western hatches. I hunted for weeks to find a guide for the Bitterroot River in western Montana. I found none. I finally located a local angler from the Missoula, Montana, area who promised to take me to the Bitterroot River for a day. I even agreed to pay him to guide me. I waited for more than an hour after I deplaned and never saw the angler. For that inaugural momentous trip to the West, I was on my own. No one to guide me—no one to tell me where to fish—no one to tell me what hatch to expect or how to match it if it appears.

What a change has occurred in the past 50 years in fly fishing! Guides can now be found on most rivers of the West. On many of the more famous rivers, you have a wide selection of guides. And most float the larger rivers. The same goes for the East and Midwest. Thirty years ago, central Pennsylvania had no guides. Now there are at least two dozen good ones, and the number keeps growing. Even by the early '90s, guides began to appear on many of the more famous rivers.

So if you want to fish the hatches and use the right pattern—and your knowledge of the stream or streams you plan to fish is limited—then hire a

Why keep a journal?

I've referred to my journals many, many times. The journal reminds me where to find specific hatches and at what times. Further, it tells me what flowers are blooming when a specific hatch is appearing. In the journal I also indicate which hatches appeared at what time and date. All of this information is useful later on and the journal constantly reminds me of the wonderful fly fishing I've experienced.

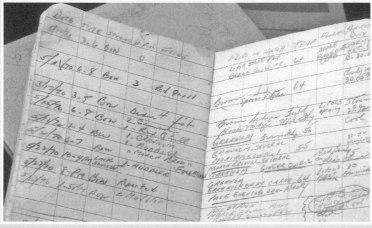

Drift boats are not only an effective way of covering lots of the best water, they are a wonderfully relaxing way to travel and enjoy the beauty of the river.

guide. Guides and drift boats help you be at the right place at the right time. Remember that the next time you can't reach the hatches.

By timing the hatches, preparing ahead of time, and being at the right place at the right time, you will have more success. Will all of this preparation guarantee that you see a hatch? No way! Warren Lentz, a legendary fly fisher on Penns Creek, said it best. He said you are going to have days when you think you've done everything right and everything goes wrong. I have planned for a hatch as well as I could and arrived on stream to find no insects emerging—or, even worse, heard later that there was a great hatch upstream! No matter how well you plan, you cannot control Mother Nature.

Match Shape and Profile

Matching the shape and profile of the many different insects you encounter on the stream is extremely important. In a short period of time, trout can switch from feeding on a mayfly, to a caddisfly, to a stonefly, to a terrestrial, to all sorts of minutiae. In addition to differences between the insects, trout often key in on differences among the same insect—trout often feed on a mayfly with upright wings or one with spent wings or move from targeting living insects to dead ones. Some insects float for long distances partially submerged or sideways (cripples) or bunch together (clusters). One of the great challenges of fly fishing is the art of imitating these different shapes and profiles.

To be effective at matching the hatch, you must match what the trout see. Remember that many duns float for long distances with one or both wings on the water.

MAYFLY PROFILES AND PATTERNS

Examine the next mayfly you see. Look at the belly, thorax, wings, and legs. First and foremost, you'll see that the body is as long as the wings. Next, even from underneath you'll note that the wings stand upright and that

> **TIP**
>
> Trout see the abdomens of insects. That's what they key on. Look at the abdomen and you often see a multicolored body.

they are important in profile. Probably the belly is lighter than the rest of the body, and it is often distinctly ribbed. As with many down-wings, the thorax is usually darker than the body. Take a close look at the thorax and you'll quickly see that unlike a Catskill-type dry fly there are no legs emanating from the bottom of the body. Inspect the fly pattern you plan to use to copy this hatch. You'll probably note that there is no ribbing on the artificial. And you can't see the thorax or neck area because of all of the hackle.

Wings

Wings create an important part of a mayfly's profile. Emerger wings look like a bump on the mesothorax of the mayfly. Imitating the immature wing can often match the hatch well. Once emerged, mayfly wings take on an upright position. Just look at some of the abdomen shots of mayflies and you'll readily see that wings are conspicuous to trout when naturals rest on the surface before takeoff. Wings come in many shapes and sizes. Mayfly wings are mostly upright and slightly slanted back toward the tail when emerging duns rest on the surface. Some can, however, be bent or malformed, and anglers call these mayflies cripples. Most duns have cloudy gray wings.

Spinners or mating adults usually have glassy, clear wings, some heavily barred, some almost without any visible veins. After a spinner lays its eggs, the wings can become spent or upright, with the former more common than the latter. Sulphur and PMD spinners, however, often rest on the surface with wings in an upright position. Stonefly and caddisfly wings when at rest are held in a down-wing configuration; that is, folded back over the body. When caddisflies lay eggs and die, their wings drop spent, which you should copy in your patterns.

Most upright wings in mayfly duns (at rest on the surface before takeoff) are not spread out like in a Catskill tie, but are closer together like in a parachute tie. These mayfly wings can be copied with mallard flank-feather fibers (if you want to emphasize a barred effect); hen-hackle wings, regular or burned; or you can use synthetic materials like poly yarn to copy wings. Poly wings are great to work with and easy to cut if you want shorter wings, especially for the Quick Trim flies discussed in chapter 7. For years mallard quill sections were more the material of choice than any others. These quill sections, however, can split or twist a fine leader and have lost favor in recent years.

An Upside-Down Lesson
On June 1, 1973, I witnessed an anomaly on the Little Juniata River that I never saw before or since. That evening on that central Pennsylvania river I saw one of the heaviest hatches of Green Drakes ever on any river at any time. About 8 p.m. the riffle and pool area in front of me came alive with struggling behemoth cream duns.

With all these large mayflies on the surface, you'd expect to see plenty of rising trout. There were none. The surface, except for the struggling duns, was void of any activity. In the next fifteen minutes I searched for escaping duns and saw none. Not one of the hundreds and hundreds of duns took flight, and no trout rose. What happened? When I examined a couple of duns closely, I noticed that all had emerged upside down and they tried to valiantly escape by flapping their wings. You think that action would have persuaded trout to feed. It didn't.

Note this mayfly's prominent upright wings. But don't be fooled. Many times the naturals do not float on the water like this— some even emerge upside down!

Why didn't trout feed on these mayflies and why did all of these mayflies emerge upside down? At that time in aquatic history the Little Juniata did not have a Green Drake hatch. Its major tributary, Spruce Creek, however, held a tremendous number of these large mayflies. The Green Drake has a two-year life cycle. That meant eggs laid in 1971 appeared on the surface as duns in 1973. On June 21, 1972, Hurricane Agnes devastated the area around the river and interrupted the life cycle of this large burrower. Fifteen inches of rain fell in five days. Spruce Creek poured its contents into the Little Juniata River. One of those contents was a large number of one-year-old Green Drake nymphs. These nymphs drifted a mile or so until they hit a pocket of slower water exactly where I fished that evening. They burrowed in this river and the following year, 1973, they emerged. This translocation evidently disoriented the mayflies and they emerged upside down. I know this area of the river held plenty of trout. Another content dumped into the flooded river was a good number of huge Spruce Creek wild brown trout.

> **TIP**
>
> Tie some sunken patterns to copy the duns and spinners of most mayflies. Sunken dun and spinner patterns really work. Fishing a sunken Trico spinner pattern on the Ruby River in Montana saved the day for me on at least two occasions. And the largest trout I ever caught during a Green Drake dun hatch was caught on a dry fly purposely sunk under the surface a few inches. If you feel you have a proper match and you haven't been catching many trout, sink the fly.

But the more important question that evening for me was why didn't the trout feed on all this easy-to-capture food? First, it's not normal for trout to see these mayflies float upside down. Remember this story when your imitation doesn't float right side up. It might be worthwhile to recast the fly so you get it riding in an upright position, or tie a new type of pattern that does float right side up.

I am certain that trout would soon get acclimated to feeding on upside-down mayflies if other hatches appeared in the same way. They readily feed on cripples during a Sulphur hatch. Those cripples have a wing missing, a nymphal shuck still attached, or legs malformed.

As a result of the Green Drake incident, as well as taking lots of pictures of the undersides of mayflies, I've arrived at four recommendations regarding mayfly imitations.

1. Trim hackle off the bottom if you're tying a classic Catskill-type pattern. After you've completed tying the pattern, take scissors and cut the hackle from the underside so your pattern floats more flush on the surface. This technique will make the fly more stable and also cut out legs (hackle) where there are none. Or, better yet, tie a parachute-type pattern or a Compara-dun-style fly, which has no hackle on the bottom.

Some fly patterns are inherently better to use to copy the shape and profile of mayflies than others. Look at a parachute pattern from underneath, and you'll immediately see that it has no hackle fibers covering the thorax. So my pattern of choice to copy an emerging mayfly dun is a parachute-type pattern. If you have no parachute flies, you can create an acceptable artificial by cutting part of the hackle fibers from the bottom. I call this a clipped-hackle fly. You can accomplish the same effect if you tie in a hackle on a down-wing fly by cutting out the hackle on the bottom. By doing this, the fly will float upright and the pattern will more closely mimic the legs of the natural.

2. Rib it! What do fly patterns like the Red Quill, Blue Quill, Quill Gordon, and Black Quill have in common? They all contain prominently ribbed bodies. Look at those photos of the abdomens and you'll see how important ribbing is. Examine a Blue Quill dun and you see how the ribbing stands out. Ribbing is evident on some insects more than others. I frequently use stripped hackle stems and eyed peacock herls to obtain the proper ribbing. Both come in a variety of dyed colors. I use an eraser to get rid of all of the fibers on eyed peacock; if I use a hackle stem, I strip the fibers. If I want an unusual ribbing color (blue, for example), I use dye.

Plain thread also makes a great ribbing material. Thread is easy to use and comes in a variety of colors.

3. Add one or two turns of the required color for the thorax or neck. Again, this difference in color is more evident in some species. For example, the Gray Caddis found on the Kootenai River in July has a black thorax. After you've completed the gray body, dub black angora and make a turn or two at the neck.

Note the prominent rib on this caddisfly's body; also, note that the wings are much longer than the body. Many fly tiers do not imitate these features.

4. Examine the tails in the abdomen shots. You'll note two things immediately: The tails are split and many are striated. I once conducted an informal test during a Trico spinnerfall. A split-tailed imitation caught

twice as many trout than a nonsplit-tailed one. Greg Smith of Wilmington, Delaware, corroborates my observations. He consistently catches more trout with a split-tailed imitation.

Cripples and Clusters

On the Little Juniata, trout refused to feed on naturals upside down on the surface. Trout, however, will readily feed on mayfly cripples and on clusters or groups of smaller flies.

The Sulphur and other members of the same genus (*Ephemerella*) often emerge with a bent wing, malformed legs, or a nymphal shuck still attached. When they emerge in this manner they are often unable to fly and are easy prey for trout. Anglers call these cripples.

A study of mayflies on Spring Creek in central Pennsylvania convinced me that trout feed on cripples. Trout often seek out these laggard mayfly duns that are unable to take flight because of an abnormality. One after-

Paul Weamer's Truform flies (above) are tied on bent hooks to imitate the natural shape of the mayfly's body. Also, the hackle is wrapped parachute-style on the bottom of the fly.

noon I stood in the middle of the stream at the tail of a pool and for a half hour captured every mayfly dun that floated past me. In every case those laggards were cripples, and many had their nymphal shucks still attached. So the profile of a shuck still attached or a malformed wing can be important in matching the hatch. While tiers try to tie a perfectly shaped fly, trout are taking cripples. What does that tell you about tying the perfect fly? Other species tend to produce an unusual number of cripples. April's Hendrickson and late May's Blue-Winged Olive dun produce plenty of cripples during a hatch.

> **TIP**
>
> If you see a lot of cripples with nymphal shucks still attached, add a removable shuck to your fly.

Sometimes, especially with finicky trout, changing the profile of your fly by adding a shuck will work. Several years ago I wrote an article for *Fly Fisherman* magazine about nymphal shucks. I added a small strip of a nylon (tannish brown) stocking at the end of the tail. I hooked the nylon strip by putting the point of the hook through the piece of stocking. I used that technique when I fished Green Drake and Sulphur hatches. This technique, or profile, worked especially well on persnickety, highly selective trout that had seen plenty of fly patterns. Use some of these nylon strips in tan, pale gray, and black to match the shuck colors of most of the common hatches. You can attach them at the stream.

In addition to copying cripples, you can also use another technique, especially to match diminutive hatches like Trico and Little Blue-Winged Olives where trout often feed on two, three, and four insects at the same time. They do this to conserve energy and also because these and other small hatches appear in great numbers.

Fishing small fly patterns is not my forte. The older I get, the more difficulty I have putting that 6X tippet through the eye of a size 24 Trico pattern. And sometimes with a hatch as small as the Trico I get frustrated when the spinnerfall covers the surface. What chance does your size 24 fly pattern have? Clusters occur when trout encounter groups of several insects in close proximity. Heavy Trico spinnerfalls create clusters of insects on the water. Even winged ants in August can create clusters because of their sheer numbers. Trout conserve energy and get more than one insect per rise. What causes clusters of insects? Numbers of insects in the mating swarm fall on to the water at one time or wind blowing the insects into groups are two causes of this eating bonanza.

The Missouri River in Montana holds a spectacular Trico spinnerfall. As my son, Bryan, and I approached the river in early August one year we saw a vortex next to the river. It looked like a dust devil only it was pale gray in color. As we drove closer to the whirlpool we realized that we were witnessing a mating flight of thousands and thousands of Tricos.

When we arrived at the river we were eager to fish this often-frustrating spinnerfall. Our guide greeted us and encouraged us to hurry since the spinnerfall had already begun. As I glanced at the surface there was barely any space void of spent spinners. In some areas spinners clung together in twos, threes, and fours. It was a great setup for a cluster pattern.

When you encounter heavy spinnerfalls of small mayflies, ants, or midges, try fishing a cluster pattern. These cluster patterns can sometimes take the frustration out of matching small hatches. Tie two tails and two pairs of wings to suggest a profile of two or three Tricos lumped together. Use a size 14 to 18 large Griffiths Gnat to copy a cluster of chironomids. Clusters, or bouquet flies, have two distinct advantages. These clusters suggest to trout that with one gulp they'll get a mouthful, and they are larger and therefore easier for the angler to tie on and see.

> **TIP**
>
> Always include a few cripple patterns in your selection. Sometimes poorly tied flies catch trout during a hatch. During a Sulphur hatch recently, I checked some of the duns lingering on the surface. I examined maybe half a dozen naturals that had failed to escape from the surface. Three of these laggards had shucks still attached, two had wings not fully formed, one had a broken leg. So why do we constantly try to tie perfect fly patterns when what the trout often feed on are imperfect naturals?

CADDISFLY PROFILES AND PATTERNS

To more closely copy a true down-wing, take a close look at the belly of a caddisfly natural. Why the belly? That's what trout see! You'll immediately note that the body is much shorter than the wings. In fact it's about half the length, and the body is often noticeably ribbed or segmented. Few patterns include these two features. There's a third feature of the caddisfly: Down-wings have no tail, but many do sport noticeable antennae. Finally, take a look at the thorax, or neck area, of the caddisfly. Often that thorax is a different color, usually darker, than the body. The Tan Caddis common on the Kootenai in July has a tan-ribbed body and a black thorax. The Deerhead Caddis pattern listed on page 64 incorporates all of the features that are important to accurately copy the shape and profile of a caddis.

And matching the shape and profile of the adult insect is not the only important consideration. You must also match the shape of the nymph and larva. Look what happened on the Ruby River several years ago.

The midsize Ruby River in southwestern Montana holds some great hatches and a good number of brown and rainbow trout, even grayling in its upper reaches. Fish the river when no hatch appears and you can become frustrated. Fish this same river when a hatch appears and you're in for some exciting fishing. The Tan Caddis is one of those great hatches on that river, and it appears nightly for a couple of weeks in August. But my son, Bryan, and I fished the stream on an early August morning when few insects appeared. I tied on a Beadhead Pheasant Tail Nymph and looked forward to a week of productive fishing. It was the first morning of our trip. Within minutes of our arrival I looked upriver and saw Bryan land a 12-inch

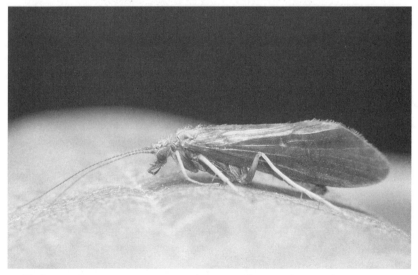

Caddisflies are important insects on a wide variety of waters, from northwest Montana's Kootenai River to Pennsylvania's Penns Creek. Just about every trout stream in the West holds a caddis hatch just about every evening throughout the summer. Bryan Meck and I fished the Kootenai for a week in late July just a year ago. Every evening around 8 p.m. caddisflies appeared. For a river that had been void of rising trout for the entire day, the caddis hatch brought hungry, eagerly feeding trout to the surface that readily took a Deerhead Tan Caddis.

rainbow. A few minutes later he landed another small fish, and in no time he had another trout on his fly. Me, I had nothing, not even a strike. For an hour this scene occurred over and over and over again. The son was out-fishing his dad by a wide margin. In that hour I managed to land one measly trout. Finally I asked him for a Tan Caddis pattern—no, I begged him for one. Within seconds after I tied that down-wing fly on to my tippet, I began to catch trout—plenty of them. It was the fly that made the difference. We caught trout all day on that Beadhead Tan Caddis pattern.

> **Tan Deerhead Caddis**
>
> **Hook:**   #12-18
> **Thread:** Tan
> **Body:**   Tan poly yarn, ribbed
>   with fine brown thread
> **Thorax:** Black poly, dubbed
> **Wing:**   Deer hair
> **Hackle:** Brown (optional)

We went back around 7 p.m. that evening to fish the Ruby again. It didn't take long to figure out why trout eagerly took the Tan Caddis wet fly earlier in the day. Shortly after we arrived in the evening, a heavy Tan Caddis hatch appeared and fish fed eagerly with their typical splashing rises.

Matching caddisflies is important almost the entire season in many areas of the United States. But as common as the down-wing hatches are over the years, I have experienced frustrating days fishing some of the common down-wing patterns. How do you tie a better down-wing pattern? Let's look at a recipe for a Tan Caddis.

1. Tie in the deer hair just behind the eye of the hook. The deer hair tips face forward and the butts face toward the bend of the hook. Clip off the butts closely. The tips of the hair should extend well beyond the eye of the hook. Make the wings as long as possible (about twice as long as the body). You can trim the wings later.

2. Next tie in a piece of fine brown thread at the bend of the hook. Use tan poly dubbed generously and wind it up to the eye, leaving plenty of space for the wing and hackle. Adding a hackle or legs is optional, but if you want to skitter the pattern, a stiff hackle will help.

3. Take the brown thread that was left at the bend of the hook and rib the body with it. Take a turn or two of black dubbing (poly) for the thorax and tie off.

4. Finally pull the wing back over the robust body. If there are any stray deer hairs facing forward, you can cut them off or leave them there as antennae. Remember to make the wings twice as long as the body.

5. Tie in a hackle at the thorax and make about five or six turns. Form a neat head. I call the finished down-wing pattern the Deerhead Caddis, a great profile for a caddisfly imitation.

A correct pattern is only part of the recipe for success when fishing these down-wings. You need to fish the pattern in the correct manner too. Leonard Wright wrote a fishing book entitled *Flutter, Skitter, and Skim* entirely devoted to moving the fly. Egg-laying caddisflies move erratically on and under the water. Trout eagerly look for that action and often feed actively on dragging flies, flies diving under the water to lay eggs, and flies moving up and down from the surface to deposit eggs. Imitate those caddisfly motions when you fish over a down-wing hatch and you'll experience

The Deerhead Caddis imitates the prominent ribbing in most adult caddisflies.

Splay the deer hair or elk wings of your stonefly or hopper patterns to suggest movement and the larger profile of the naturals.

more success. In a later chapter I mention an experiment with the Green Caddis hatch. In that experiment you'll see that I caught twice as many trout when I moved the fly.

ANT AND OTHER TERRESTRIAL PROFILES

Is the profile of an ant important to copy? Recently I fished with Bill Gamber, one of the most innovative fly fishers I know. Bill fished for more than two hours and landed just one trout. We both saw trout rising, but no trout rose to the flies we offered. That is, until Bill tied on a winged ant. It was late August, a time of year when ants form new colonies. Many of these winged ants land on the surface of trout streams and fish often and regularly feed on them. Bill fished all kinds of patterns, but until he fished a two-humped wing ant he had little success. After he tied on that winged ant, he caught five trout in half an hour. In that 200-foot section of stream, every trout that rose took Bill's pattern.

The profile for grasshoppers and terrestrials other than the ant can also be important to copy. A hopper pattern caught trout for me in the Browns Canyon section of Colorado's Arkansas River. As with the caddis, sometimes moving the pattern means the difference between success and frustration. Trout eagerly took the moving hopper on the Arkansas.

The late Ken Sink once invited me to fish with him on some private water. He had a long ladder in the back of the truck, and I asked what that ladder was for. He said that I'd find out soon enough. When we arrived at the stream, Ken headed for the back of the truck, pulled out the ladder, and placed it against a high tree near the creek.

"One of my flies is up on that branch. Try to get it for me," he said.

I was much younger then, and I climbed the ladder and retrieved his fly. I gave the fly a good look and saw it was a hopper pattern. That fly had caught many trout for Ken the day before, and it was the only copy of the yellow-bodied pattern that he had. To this day I call the fly Ken's Hopper. The profile of that fly looked similar to the local grasshoppers, and that fly that I retrieved from the tree caught trout for Ken all day.

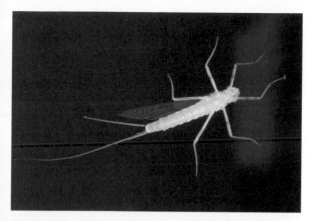

The abdomen of a female Light Cahill spinner (*Stenacron interpunctatum*). Note the orange shading.

An eastern Speckle-Winged Spinner (*Callibaetis*). The spinnerfall can create some great surface feeding on still waters much of the fishing season.

A male Trico spinner. Note the fine white ribbing on the abdomen.

Montana's Madison River in July. Look for the Salmonfly early in the month on this productive river.

Bodies of Quick Trim flies can be made from vernille (left), thin foam strips (center), or closed cell packing strips (right). Color and cut the body and wings to copy the size of the hatch.

Henry's Fork in eastern Idaho is an insect factory. In June and July look for Blue-Winged Flavs and Gray and Brown Drakes. Cloudy days or low light often produce the best hatches.

A Light Cahill dun (*Stenacron interpunctatum*). Duns appear in late May and early June in the evening.

A White Fly (*Ephoron leukon*) male spinner. Only the male changes from a dun to a spinner. PAUL WEAMER PHOTO

The October Caddis appears in early October. Look for the hatch to appear in the late afternoon and early evening.

A Gray Fox (*Maccaffertium Ithaca*). Look for the hatch to appear after the March Brown.

A female Sulphur Dun (*Ephemerella invaria*). Heavy hatches appear in mid to late May in the East and Midwest.

A Blue-Winged Olive from the "Run"—the outflow of Boiling Springs Lake that flows into the Yellow Breeches in Boiling Springs, Pennsylvania. BWOs can hatch at any time of the year here.

Above: Mike Lawson's Paradrake pattern caught this cutthroat on the Big Hole River in Montana—even when no drakes were hatching.

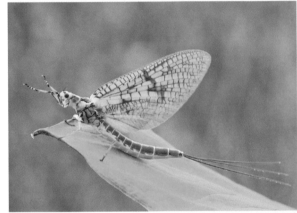

Eastern Green Drake.

Down-wing hatches like this Grannom caddis are important much of the fishing season. Try tying some using the Deerhead Caddis pattern. JAY NICHOLS PHOTO

Golden Stone from Pine Creek, Pennsylvania. Note how the wings lay flat.

Spinners present a pronounced profile to the trout. The spent wings signal an easy meal.

PMDs vary in color tremendously from stream to stream, even on the same water. This one with a pinkish body is from the Taylor River in Colorado.

Above: Spring Creek in central Pennsylvania holds a heavy Sulphur hatch. Expect heavy fishing pressure during this hatch in mid and late May.

Quick Trim flies are easy to tie and easy to trim—quickly. Just take a permanent marking pen and color the body and wings the appropriate color, and then trim to match the size of the hatch.

Be Creative and Unorthodox

nterest in fly fishing has increased over the years, which has meant plenty of added fishing pressure on our favorite streams and rivers and many more highly selective trout. Add a well-known hatch to the picture and you have even more anglers to contend with. Because of the pressure and increasingly savvy fish, you must take advantage of every possible technique, odd as it may seem at the time, to catch fish under difficult conditions.

There are many tactics you can resort to when a hatch appears and you become frustrated—you can sink the dry fly, add a shuck to the fly, move or impart motion to the fly, or change the color of the fly. We'll explore all of these strategies and more to help you catch more trout.

Sometimes it pays to use unorthodox techniques such as sinking your dry fly or fishing something entirely different than what the fish are feeding on.

SINK THAT FLY

If you don't catch trout on the dry fly you are using, purposely pull it underneath the surface and fish it there. This tactic first solved the riddle of trout feeding on sunken Trico spinners for me, but I have since used it countless times to catch fish in tough conditions. Sinking the fly has worked so often for me that it's now second nature to sink the dry fly dun or spinner imitation if I feel I have a correct match. In fact, add some weight to some of your dun and spinner patterns so they sink more quickly. So remember, if you have matched a hatch and trout aren't taking your fly, then sink that pattern—spinner or dun—and fish it underneath. With the dun pattern, try imparting some motion to the fly to suggest emergence. With a spinner pattern, fish it on a dead drift.

Sinking the pattern not only works during a spinnerfall, but also when duns appear. That same tactic has worked when Green Drakes appeared on famous limestone streams like Penns, Spruce, and Big Fishing creeks in central Pennsylvania; and Yellow Creek in southwestern Pennsylvania. On Penns Creek one evening I hadn't caught a trout and the hatch had already appeared for more than an hour. Finally, in a desperate move, I jerked my large Green Drake dry fly so it drifted a few inches under the surface. On the very first cast I hooked a 19-inch brown trout. I continued that technique for the next hour and landed two more trout. The same technique worked on the Sinnemahoning Creek just upstream from Emporium in north central Pennsylvania. Craig Hudson, Don Perry, Tom Barton, and Mark Campbell wanted to show me the Green Drake hatch. Drakes emerged throughout the fly-fishing-only project, but so far we were shut out. Then Don Perry yelled out, "They're taking a sunken Green Drake." So the five of us purposely tugged our dry flies under the surface just upstream from feeding trout. It didn't take long to prove the merits of this technique for feeding trout, and we all ended the evening satisfied that sinking that Green Drake pattern saved the day.

> **TIP**
>
> Tie larger patterns like a cluster, or bouquet, for smaller, dense hatches. That becomes important especially if you are an older fly fisher.

Hatches like the Green Drake (*Ephemera guttulata*), Hendrickson (*Ephemerella subvaria*), and Western March Brown (*Rhithrogena morrisoni*) and spinners like the Coffin Fly (*Ephemera guttulata*) and the Red Quill (*Ephemerella subvaria*) work well sunken.

Trout can be spooky in clear water and may not rise to take your dry fly. In this situation, you might try dropping a Zebra Midge or other small nymph off the back of your dry.

MOVE THE FLY

From the beginning, fly fishers are taught to present the fly drag-free. The fly must drift at a speed equal to the flotsam on the surface if you want to catch more trout. But on many occasions, moving or dragging the dry fly works more effectively than a dead drift—especially with caddis hatches.

When I recently asked Warren Lentz what the top two hatches were on Penns Creek, he listed the Green Drake as number one, but he surprised me with his second top hatch on that stream, a down-wing, the Grannom. So caddisflies can be important anywhere you fish.

Whether you are using a wet or dry fly, often the only way to get strikes while fishing a caddis hatch is to drag the fly. I recently watched Jay Nichols fish a Tan Caddis in this method. He tied on a long, 15-foot fine leader and skittered the down-wing dry fly across the surface. In a short time he picked up a half dozen trout with this method of fishing. If normal drag-free fishing doesn't work, try this method, especially if you are fishing over caddis egg layers.

Often twitching a down-wing wet fly catches trout when a drag-free drift doesn't. It was more than 20 years ago that central Pennsylvania's Little Juniata River held its last spectacular Green Caddis hatch. In more recent years, that hatch has been supplanted by an enormous Grannom hatch that lasts for a week or more. During the week the Green Caddis hatch appeared in heavy numbers, I conducted an experiment. I cast a Green Caddis wet fly 2,000 times using a counter and keeping a record. On half of those casts I fished the fly on a dead drift. On the other half I twitched or moved the fly. All experiments occurred while actual Green Caddis naturals were emerging. With the dead drift, I had 30 strikes on 1,000 casts. When I twitched or moved the fly, I had 63, or more than twice the number of strikes.

What does this experiment prove? During a caddisfly hatch, you should move your wet fly. If you're fishing a dry fly, try skittering it across the surface or in fast water.

Skating your dry fly across the surface often works to entice fish. To perform this technique, make sure your flies have plenty of floatant (liquid or dry) on them and you use a long leader.

But moving or twitching the fly doesn't end there. It also sometimes works when fishing mayfly imitations. Recently I fished with Bill Gamber, Ken Kreider, and Larry Goff during a Green Drake hatch. Green Drakes are large. In fact, they're huge as mayflies go. Duns often have difficulty taking flight and struggle on the surface before they actually become airborne. I sat back and watched the hatch progress and noted that the more the duns struggled on the surface, the more violently the trout struck them. I suggested to Larry and Ken that they twitch or move their dry-fly imitations. On the first cast a heavy trout struck Larry's drake pattern. For the next hour the two caught more than a half dozen trout—all on a moving dry fly.

> ### TIP
> On occasion when a drag-free drift doesn't work, try dragging or moving the dry or wet fly. This often works with larger hatches (like the Green Drake) and caddisfly hatches.

And Bob Budd and I have even more experiences with moving a dry fly. Bob is probably the best dry-fly fisherman that I have ever fished with. Both of us fished the White Fly hatches for several years on the Little Juniata River. (That hatch has diminished in the past few years.) One evening Bob and I decided to move upstream to a pod of rising trout. Bob put his fly rod over his shoulder and proceeded to head up to the rising fish. As he moved upriver, his White Fly pattern dragged behind him and a trout struck the dragging fly. After that incident, and when I fish the White Fly hatch especially, I drag the floating fly a foot upstream from a trout rising to White Fly naturals. Dragging or twitching the imitation during a White Fly hatch often results in strikes.

FISH A SMALLER OR TOTALLY DIFFERENT FLY

On Colorado's South Platte River just below Spinney Reservoir, the trout are huge, and they are so familiar with fly fishers that they feed within feet of casting anglers. The first generation of Tricos on the South Platte is often larger than the second generation. These trout have seen every pattern imaginable. When Phil Camera and I fished the river more than a decade ago, we tied on a size 24, slightly smaller than the natural. Although many trout still ignored the smaller fly, we were rewarded with plenty of strikes. Remember when fishing heavily fished waters sporting a hatch, try a fly smaller than the natural.

ADD A SHUCK

Have you ever watched a nymph change into a dun? Have you ever noticed a Sulphur or PMD cripple on the surface? These cripples are the most available for trout because they are unable to take off, and trout readily feed on them. Check some of these cripples and you'll see many still have the shuck still attached, which prevents them from taking flight.

To be prepared, tie a few patterns with a shuck attached to the fly where the tail is tied in. You can tie in shucks as you're tying the fly. Just tie in a piece of Z-Lon that is the length of the shank of the hook. Use the appropriate color to copy the nymph. Or you can cut pieces of a nylon stocking in gray, tan, or dark brown and attach them to the dry fly when a hatch appears. Use the color and size that most accurately copies the actual nymphal shuck. Attach them through the point of the hook.

This brookie rushed a large Royal Wulff after other flies failed to get its attention.

Stillwater fishing can be frustratingly difficult at times, but fishing up to three flies can help you cover different levels and find feeding fish.

UNMATCHING THE HATCH

Then there are times matching the hatch doesn't seem to work. Especially if the water is filled with duns or spinners, using something quite different might bring a strike. That's where an attractor might work. Several times during a hatch I've kept a Patriot on the leader to see if I could catch trout with it. It works—not every time mind you. Try the attractor first in a size comparable to the hatch, and if that doesn't work, try a larger size. I've caught trout on a size 12 Patriot dry fly while they fed on a Trico spinnerfall.

> **TIP**
>
> On heavily fished streams, try fishing a size smaller than the mayfly natural.

Rig Multiple Flies

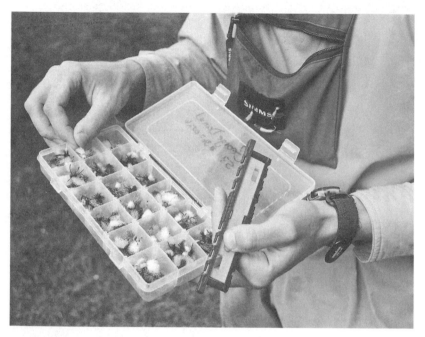

For the first 20 years of my fly-fishing life, I was a confirmed dry-fly angler. In fact, in *Meeting and Fishing the Hatches* published in 1977 I wrote: "As you read this book, you'll almost immediately note a strong personal bias on my part. I find that enticing a trout to the surface with a lifelike dry fly is much more enjoyable, rewarding, and challenging than any other type of fishing." Boy, has my thinking changed in the past 30 years. No longer am I a committed dry-fly fisherman. Even when the hatches appear, I often use a wet and a dry fly in a tandem rig. I estimate that using this type arrangement of flies has at a minimum doubled my catch. Now it's an exception rather than the rule for me to fish a dry fly

The Orvis dry-and-dropper holder, or similar devices, allow you to pre-rig multiple-fly setups so that you have them ready on the water.

only. The tandem will do the same for you. How did I get started with this technique?

It first happened on the McKenzie River just outside Eugene, Oregon, more than 20 years ago. We looked forward eagerly for a day of fishing and matching the hatches. The famous Western March Brown had already appeared on the river for the past month, and today it was expected to appear again. Our guide for the day, Ken Helfrich, tied on a special rig for Mike Manfredo and me. He tied on a March Brown wet fly as the point fly and a March Brown dry fly on a dropper as the lead fly. The dry fly floated high on the surface and acted as a strike indicator to alert us to a trout hitting the underneath fly—the wet fly. This was a first; I had never used this rig before. The hatch appeared as predicted in the early afternoon, and in the riffle and pool through which we drifted, we fished to dozens of trout rising to laggard duns on the surface and others feeding on nymphs and emergers. That hour of matching the hatch that day on the McKenzie River changed my way of fishing for the rest of my fishing life.

> **TIP**
>
> If you are not sure what phase of the mayfly trout are taking, try fishing a tandem during a hatch. Are they taking the Sulphur nymph, dun, or spinner? Fish all three at once.

The incident in Oregon was reinforced on a trip to the productive Bighorn River in Montana the next year. This time Richie Montella was our guide, and he floated us through hordes of PMD spinners. After the fall had ended, he tied on a tandem rig consisting of a PMD dun and a nymph. He connected the two in a different manner. He connected the nymph in the regular method tied on to a two-foot piece of tippet. On the other end of that tippet he tied an improved clinch knot and slipped the loop of the knot through the point of the hook of the dry fly. Anglers call this method of connecting two flies a bend connection.

Those two fishing events occurred on Western waters. Fly fishers in the West have used tandem rigs for years. But few in the East and Midwest used the rig. After two successful fishing events with the rig I decided to try it on some of the Eastern waters. Guess what? This system worked as well there as it did in the West. I'm a mediocre wet-fly fisher at best, but fishing the tandem improved dramatically my wet-fly fishing skills.

But more than just a dry fly and a wet fly, the tandem can be used to match the hatches. What are the fish taking? How many times have you asked yourself that frustrating question when you saw trout rise? Are they taking the mayfly dun, spinner, nymph, emerger, or a stonefly, caddisfly, midge, or terrestrial? What would happen if you were able to fish two or even three flies at the same time? For instance, would a rig consisting of a dun, nymph, and emerger pattern work? For one May after another, Sulphur duns and spinners have baffled me, and for years I've asked the same question: Will the dun or spinner be more important trout food that evening? Fishing a tandem rig consisting of two, three, or even four patterns at the same time can reduce tremendously your frustration when hatches appear. The tandem helps you decide what patterns to use and what flies trout are taking.

One unique advantage to fishing a tandem made up of a dry fly and one or two wet flies is that the dry fly acts as a strike indicator. Remember that bobber or floater you used as a kid—that's what the dry fly does for you. It's the only type of strike indicator on which you can catch trout. I call it a strike indicator with an attitude. I once showed the legendary fly fisher George Harvey the rig and how easy it was to use; he walked away shaking his head.

Can fishing the tandem help you become a better fly fisher? It did for me. It has doubled the average number of trout I catch. And it works just as

In low, clear water, or when fishing over spooky trout, a dry fly is often the best choice of strike indicator. It lands softly and looks a lot more natural on the surface of the water than a colored piece of foam or plastic.

well for other anglers. It's the exception rather than the rule now for anglers in the East and Midwest to fish the tandem as matter of choice. The tandem is really an effective technique. But it can even be more productive when you encounter a hatch.

TYPES OF CONNECTIONS

There are at least seven methods of connecting these flies in a tandem rig. *Fishing Tandem Flies* describes all of these. The easiest and fastest for most people is the bend connection.

Use a Tandem during a Hatch

The tandem has become a valuable tool for matching hatches. On more occasions than I can recall, I've fished the tandem with a dry fly that copies the dun and a wet fly that looks like the nymph or emerger. I call using two patterns in this manner the bi-cycle. You can tie in a Sulphur nymph as the point fly or deep fly and a Sulphur dun as the lead fly. Add weight to the nymph when you tie the fly, but never add weight to the tippet or leader. Adding lead or a small shot tends to tangle the line much quicker when you use a tandem rig.

Does the bi-cycle work during a hatch? Look at this hatch event: My son, Bryan, and I fished south central Pennsylvania's Yellow Breeches Creek in late August several years ago. At that time of year, the Yellow Breeches hosts hordes of fly fishers because of the famous White Fly hatch. The White Fly appears on the stream each evening for more than two weeks and is one of the last great hatches of the fly-fishing season. The hatch begins around 7:30 p.m. and often continues well after dark. Bryan and I both tied on a White Fly dry, and a foot or two behind that dry fly we tied on a pale gray weighted White Fly Nymph. As the easy-to-see White Fly dry fly floated in full view, the weighted nymph drifted on or near the bottom.

> **TIP**
>
> Try an unconventional pattern like an orange egg sac to copy the eggs of the Sulphur spinner. Tie some egg patterns in dark olive, orange, and white on size 16, 18, and 20 hooks. Fish the pattern behind a larger dry fly in a tandem arrangement.

The hatch began, and anglers crowded in on us. It was like opening day all over again, only this was near the end of the season. Within a hundred feet, three other anglers cast to rising trout. It didn't take long to prove the merits of the tandem during that hatch. That bi-cycle caught plenty of trout

Dry/dropper rigs are effective when flows get low and clear and trout become suspicious of standard two-fly nymphing rigs.

that evening. Bryan and I caught a dozen trout on that rig during that intense, prolific hatch. That White Fly dry fly was easier to follow even in the half-light when the hatch peaked. Twelve trout might not seem like a lot to you, but with the intense fishing pressure on the Yellow Breeches during that hatch it is quite an accomplishment.

We compared notes after the hatch had ended and estimated that we caught nine brown trout on the nymph and only three on the dry fly. What does that prove? As with so many hatches, trout feed on the nymph or emerger much more than they do on the dun on the surface. That's why the bi-cycle setup is so important.

The same bi-cycle arrangement performed well during a recent Coffin Fly spinnerfall. After an hour of futile fishing on north central Pennsylvania's Pine Creek when plenty of trout rose, I finally figured out that those highly selective fish fed on spinners that had sunken just beneath the surface. I tied on a spinner as the point fly and a Green Drake dun as the lead fly. The two were connected with a bend connection just six inches apart. The Coffin Fly sank just beneath the surface while the Green Drake floated. I twitched the duo so the spinner pattern sank just beneath the surface. It worked! Just about every trout that fed that evening hit that sunken spinner.

If you're really brave, choose a dry fly, then tie an emerger below that and a nymph below the emerger. When I use three that copy the dun, emerger, and nymph I call it the tri-cycle tandem. If you think casting two might be difficult, then try casting three at the same time. Practice casting three flies before you try it in the stream. By using three—if local fishing laws allow you to use that many—you can really take some of the guesswork out of pattern selection. For example, if you were to fish the Quill Gordon hatch in early April, you might fish the nymph as the point fly (farthest from the reel), the wet fly copying the dun as you middle fly, and a size 12 dry fly as your lead fly (nearest the reel). Add a lighter wing (white or pale gray poly yarn rather than the wood-duck wing) to make the dry fly easier to see. The possibilities in using three flies are endless, and this tandem rig should help you cope with challenging hatch situations.

This same setup works if you hit a multiple-hatch situation. For example, on several occasions I've hit hatches of Little Blue-Winged Olives and Blue Quills, almost in equal numbers, vying for the attention of feeding trout. Tie two dry flies and you're ready for both hatches.

Often the Green Drake appears simultaneously with the Sulphur. Some trout feed on the Green Drakes, but others on the smaller Sulphur. Why not construct a tandem made up of a Sulphur point fly and a Green Drake lead fly? That way you take the guesswork out of which trout is taking which fly.

You don't have to use or include a dry fly as your lead fly. Instead you can use three wet flies—also a terrific way to fish the hatches. You can even use three dry flies. Use a true tri-cycle: a nymph, an emerger, and a sunken dun.

We examined life cycles, emergers, hatch charts, and patterns in depth in an earlier chapter because they are key to your success—even with the tandem. In the hatch chart on page 84, you'll see T, B, or S listed for all of the mayflies. "T" suggests that the mayfly emerges near the top or surface. "B" indicates that the emerger transforms near the bottom, and "S" implies that the nymph swims to shore or an exposed area to emerge—usually out of the water.

> **TIP**
>
> If you have trouble following small flies during a hatch or spinnerfall (size 24 or 26, for example), use a large dry fly and tie the smaller fly as your point fly.

The majority of anglers fish all their emerger patterns near the surface, but a great number of mayflies swim to shore or change from nymph to dun at or near the bottom. For those that emerge near the bottom, fish your emerger pattern where they emerge—near the bottom. To copy those mayfly nymphs that swim to shore or to an exposed rock, try moving or twitching the pattern. So when you copy the nymph,

Guide Eric Stroup often fishes a soft-hackle wet fly at the top of his multiple-fly rig to imitate an emerging mayfly or caddis.

emerger, and dun in a bi-cycle or tri-cycle arrangement, it's important to know where the hatch you're copying changes and to fish your fly at the proper depth. If for instance, you're fishing a Quill Gordon hatch, place the wet fly as your point fly and the dry as your lead fly. Fish the point fly on or near the bottom, exactly where the dun emerges from the nymphal shuck. If you use a dry fly as your lead fly (fly nearest the reel), the fly acts as a strike indicator and quickly tells you if you have a strike on any sunken pattern you're using (see the hatch chart on page 84).

Does this bi-cycle work in the heat of a hatch? Recently I fished with Oren "B. J." Kauffman and David Scott Vlad while a Sulphur hatch emerged. Both had a three-day pass from Fort Drum, and both are avid and devoted fly fishers. First, they used a Sulphur dry and in a half hour had two strikes. Both became frustrated with the paucity of strikes during the hatch and agreed to fish a tandem composed of a Sulphur dry fly and a Beadhead Pheasant Tail nymph. (See tying instructions later in this chapter.) In the next 40 minutes, B. J. landed about 15 trout—13 on the nymph and two on the dry fly. He continued to catch trout well after dark and well after the hatch had ended. The very next evening, and again with a Sulphur hatch evident, both B. J. and Scott landed a total of 31 trout using the same tandem rig. B. J. even had a double, a rarity, on the tandem setup.

HATCH CHART

Insect	Pattern Size	Scientific Name	Region
American March Brown	#12	*Maccaffertium vicarium*	E, M
Autumn Sedge	#12	*Neophylax* spp.	E, M
Big Slate Drake Brown Drake Spinner	#8	*Hexagenia atrocaudata*	E, M
Black Quill Early Brown Spinner	#12	*Leptophlebia cupida*	E, M
Blue Dun	#20	*Iswaeon anoka*	A
Blue Quill Dark Brown Spinner	#18	*Paraleptophlebia adoptiva*	E, M
Blue Quill	#18	*Paraleptophlebia bicornuta*	W
Blue Quill Dark Brown Spinner, female	#18	*Paraleptophlebia guttata*	E, M
Blue Quill	#18	*Paraleptophlebia memorialis*	W
Blue Quill	#18	*Paraleptophlebia memorialis*	W
Blue Quill	#18	*Paraleptophlebia mollis*	E, M
Blue-Winged Olive Dun	#20	*Dannella simplex*	E, M
Blue-Winged Olive Dun Dark Olive Spinner	#14	*Drunella cornuta*	E, M
Blue-Winged Olive Dun	#16	*Drunella cornutella*	E, M
Blue-Winged Olive Dun	#14	*Drunella flavilinea*	W
Brown Drake	#10-12	*Ephemera simulans*	E, M, W, L

Key to hatch chart

Region: East (E), Midwest (M), West (W), Alaska (A), Labrador (L), or All (all areas).

Date: Approximate emergence date; can vary year to year depending on weather conditions.

Time of Day and Concentration: Morning (M), Early Afternoon (EA), Afternoon (A), or Evening (E), plus whether the hatch is concentrated (C) or sporadic (S).

Area of Emergence: Where in the stream the nymph changes to dun; useful when fishing a tandem rig. S= Swims to shore or an exposed rock, B= changes from nymph to dun near the bottom, T= changes from nymph to dun on or near the surface, M= changes near the middle depth of the stream or lakes, O= often changes out of the stream on a rock or a bridge.

Date	Time of Day and Concentration	Area of Emergence	Speed of Water and Nymph Habitat
5/20	A, E (spinner); S	T	F, M; R
9/15	A; C	B	F; R
8/15	E; C	T	S; B
4/22	A; S	S	S; F
5/5	A;	B	S, M; F
4/15	A; C	S	A; F
9/1	M, E; C	T	A; F
6/25	M, A; C	T	A; F
4/15	M;C	S	A; F
5/15	M; C	S	A; F
5/26	M, A; C	S	A; F
6/15	M (dun), E (spinner); C	B	M; F
5/25	M (dun), E (spinner);C	B	A; F
6/10	M, A; C	B	A; F
5/30	M, E; C	B	M, F; F
5/25	E; C	T	S, M; B

Nymph Habitat: Two entries in the same column. The first is the water speed the nymph prefers: S= Slow, M= Moderate, F= Fast, A= All types. The second indicates whether the nymph lives on rocks, is free swimming, lives on weeds or vegetation, is cased, or burrows or lives in detritus: R = Rocks, F = Free-swimming, V = Vegetation, C = Cased, B= Burrows.

Table Footnotes:
     *Later on inland waters.
   **More than one generation per year.
  ***Hatches can appear into June.
   +Appears in February in the Southwest (Arizona).

HATCH CHART continued

Insect	Pattern Size	Scientific Name	Region
Chocolate Dun, male Olive Sulphur, female	#16	Ephemerella needhami	E, M
Chocolate Dun	#16-18	Eurylophella bicolor	E, M
Cream Cahill	#14-16	Maccaffertium modestum	E, M
Cream Cahill	#14	Maccaffertium pulchellum	E, M
Dark Blue Quill	#16	Teloganopsis deficiens	E, M
Dark Blue Sedge	#14	Psilotreta frontalis	E, M
Dark Brown Dun	#14	Ameletus cooki	W
Dark Brown Dun	#20	Diphetor hageni	W
Dark Green Drake	#10	Litobrancha recurvata	E, M
Dark Olive Dun	#12	Siphloplecton basale	E, M, L
Dark Quill Gordon	#12	Ameletus ludens	E, M
Early Brown Stonefly	#12-14	Strophopteryx fasciata	E, M
Golden Drake	#12	Anthopotamus distinctus	E
Golden Stonefly	#8	Calineuria californica	W
Grannom	#12-16	Brachycentrus fuliginosus	E, M
Grannom	#12-14	Brachycentrus numerosus	E
Gray Drake	#12	Siphlonurus occidentalis	W
Gray Drake	#12-14	Siphlonurus quebecensis	E, M
Gray Fox	#14	Heptagenia solitaria	W
Green Caddis	#14	Rhyacophila lobifera	E, M
Green Drake Coffin Fly	#8-10	Ephemera guttulata	E
Green Drake	#10	Hexagenia rigida	E, M, L
Light Cahill	#12	Cinygma dimicki	W
Light Cahill	#12	Heptagenia marginalis	E, M
Light Cahill	#14	Maccaffertium ithaca	E

Date	Time of Day and Concentration	Area of Emergence	Speed of Water and Nymph Habitat
5/30	M (dun), E(spinner); C	T	M; V
5/22	A (dun), E (spinner); C	B	M, F; F
8/1	E; C	T	M, F; R
6/15	E; S	T	M, F; R
5/26	EE; C	T	S, M; F
6/1	E; C	B	F
7/10	M, A; C	B	M, F; R
6/15	M, A; C	B	M; F
5/25	A (dun), E (spinner); C, S	T	S; B
4/20	EA;C	T	S, M; V
4/18	A; C	S, O	M, F; F
4/10	A; S	O	M, F; R
6/25	E; C	B	S, M; B
6/1	M; S	O	F; R
4/22	A; C	B	S, M; C
4/22	A; C	B	S, M; C
7/1	A; C	S	S; F
5/25	M, A, E (dun), E (spinner); C	S	S; F
7/1	E; C	T	F, M; R
5/8	A; C	B	F; F
5/25	E; C	T	S, M; B
6/15	E; C	T	S; B
6/15	E; S	T	S, M; R
6/15	E; S	T	M, F; R
5/25	E; C	T	M, F; R

HATCH CHART continued

Insect	Pattern Size	Scientific Name	Region
Light Cahill	#12-14	Stenacron interpunctatum	E, M
Light Stonefly	#12	Isoperla signata	E, M
Little Black Caddis	#14	Chimarra aterrima	E, M
Little Black Stonefly	#14-18	Capnia vernalis	E, M, W
Little Blue-Winged Olive Dun	#20	Baetis bicaudatus	W
Little Blue-Winged Olive Dun	#20	Baetis brunneicolor	W
Little Blue-Winged Olive Dun Rusty Spinner	#20	Baetis intercalaris	E, M, W
Little Blue-Winged Olive Dun Rusty Spinner	#20	Baetis tricaudatus**	E, M, W
Little Blue-Winged Olive Dun	#20	Baetis tricaudatus	E, M, W
Little Blue-Winged Olive Dun	#20	Plauditus veteris	E, M, W
Little Golden Stonefly	#16	Suwallia pallidula	W
Little Olive Dun spinner	#20-24	Tricorythodes fictus	W
Little Olive Dun spinner	#24	Tricorythodes allectus, T. atratus	E, M
Little Olive Dun	#24	Tricorythodes explicates, T. spp.	W
Little Olive Dun	#24	Tricorythodes stygiatus, T. spp.	E, M
Little White Mayfly	#24-26	Caenis latipennis	All
Mother's Day Caddis	#14-16	Brachycentrus occidentalis	W
Pale Brown Dun	#14	Cinygmula reticulata	W
Pale Brown Dun	#14	Rhithrogena hageni	W
Pale Evening Dun	#18	Ephemerella dorothea dorothea	E, M
Pale Evening Dun	#14	Heptagenia elegantula	W
Pale Evening Dun	#16	Leucrocuta aphrodite	E
Pale Evening Dun	#16	Leucrocuta hebe	E, M
Pale Evening Dun	#14-16	Penelomax septentrionalis	E, M

Date	Time of Day and Concentration	Area of Emergence	Speed of Water and Nymph Habitat
5/25	E; C	T	M, F; R
5/8	A; S	O	F; R
4/20	A; C	B	F; R
2/1	A; S	O	M, F; R
5/20	A; C	T	F
5/15	A; C	T	A; F
3/10, 9/1	A; C	T	M, F; F
4/1	A; C	T	M, F; F
9/1**	A (dun, spinner), E (spinner); C	T	A; F
9/1	A; C	T	A; F
4/1	A; C	O	F; R
2/15**+	M; C	S, B	S; F
7/1	M; C	S, B	S; F
7/1	M; C	S, B	S; F
7/1	M; C	S, B	S; F
6/15	E (dun), M (spinner); C	T	S; F
5/1	A; C	B	S, M; C
7/5	M, A; S	T	F
7/10	M, A; C	T	M, F; R
5/31	E; C	T, M	M; F
6/ 15	E; C	T	S, M; R
5/20	E; C	T	F; R
6/22	E; S	T	M, F;
5/18	E; C	B	F, M; F

HATCH CHART continued

Insect	Pattern Size	Scientific Name	Region
Pale Morning Dun	#18	Ephemerella dorothea infrequens	W
Pale Morning Dun	#16	Ephemerella excrucians (formerly inermis)	W, A
Pink Cahill, female Light Cahill, male	#14	Epeorus vitreus	E, M
Pink Lady	#12	Epeorus albertae	W
Quill Gordon	#14-16	Epeorus longimanus	W
Quill Gordon Red Quill Spinner	#14	Epeorus pleuralis	E
Quill Gordon	#12	Rhithrogena futilis, R. undulata	W
Quill Gordon	#12	Rhithrogena undulata	W
Red Quill, male Hendrickson, female Red Quill Spinner	#14-16	Ephemerella subvaria	E, M
Salmonfly	#8	Pteronarcys californica	W
Slate Drake	#12	Isonychia bicolor	E, M
Slate Drake	#14	Isonychia bicolor	E, M
Speckle-Winged Dun	#14	Callibaetis ferrugineus hageni	W
Speckle-Winged Dun Speckle-Winged Spinner	#14	Callibaetis skokianus**	E, M
Spotted Sedge	#14	Symphitopsyche slossanae	E, M
Sulphur Sulphur spinner	#15	Ephemerella invaria (now includes rotunda)	E, M
Western Green Drake	#10-12	Drunella grandis grandis	W
Western March Brown	#14	Rhithrogena morrisoni	W
White Fly	#14	Ephoron album	W
White Fly	#14	Ephoron leukon	E, M
Yellow Drake	#12	Ephemera varia	E, M

Date	Time of Day and Concentration	Area of Emergence	Speed of Water and Nymph Habitat
5/20	M; C	T, M	M; F
5/20	M, A, E; C	T, M	A; F
5/25**	E; C	B	M, F; R
6/25	E; C	B	M; R
4/1–6/30	A; C	B	M, F; R
4/15***	A; C	B	F; R
6/25	M, A; S	T	F; R
7/10	M, A; C	T	M, F; R
4/20	A; C	B	A; R
5/20	M; S	O	F; R
5/25**	E; C, S	S	M, F; F
9/1**	A, E; S	S	F; F
5/1	M, A; C	T	S; F (prefers alkaline lakes)
4/10	M, A; S	B	S; F (prefers alkaline lakes)
5/23	A; C	B	M; F
5/8	E; C	T, M	M, F; R
5/20	M; C	B	M; F
2/25*	A; C	T	M, F; R
8/15	E; C	T	M; B
8/12	E; C	T	M; B
6/15	E; C	T	S; B

One of my go-to setups is a Patriot dry fly with a Zebra Midge dropper. That rig has worked for me on waters across the country.

There's still another important way you can incorporate the tandem into your fishing regime. This method works on tiny hatches like the Trico and Little-Blue-Winged Olive. If you have trouble following small flies on the surface, try this. Tie the Trico or other small fly matching the hatch as the point fly (farther from the reel) and a larger, easier to follow attractor like the Patriot two feet in front (nearer the reel) of the smaller fly. This way you'll have a good idea where your smaller fly is. I've used this technique many times, and I have caught trout on the Trico and on the attractor pattern. Better yet, you can tie on a weighted Trico as your point fly and a size 12 to 16 Patriot as your dry fly. This technique, where the Trico spinner sinks beneath the surface, seems to work on heavily fished trout streams.

Quite often you'll encounter trout feeding exclusively on midges. I hit such a hatch with plenty of rising trout onc early November. It appeared that trout fed just under the surface late that afternoon, so I tied on a size 12 Patriot dry fly as the lead fly and just six inches behind the dry fly I tied on a size 20 Zebra Midge. That midge drifted just a few inches under the surface. More than 20 trout took that Zebra Midge on that trip.

In *How to Catch More Trout* I said that one important ingredient for catching more trout is depth. If trout are feeding on or near the bottom, fish your fly there. There's no better way of fishing depth correctly than using the tandem rig. If the trout are feeding near the bottom, then increase the distance between your dry fly and wet fly. If fish are feeding just under the surface, then shorten the distance between the two.

I said earlier that I have encountered multiple hatches when some trout are feeding on one insect and other trout on another insect. It happened in the East with the Green Drake and Sulphur and the Blue Quill and Little Blue-Winged Olive; and with the Blue-Winged Olive, Green Drake, and Pale Morning Dun in the West. Tie on a large Green Drake as the lead fly and the smaller Sulphur dry fly as the point fly. Or as I mentioned before, tie on a Sulphur dun and spinner in a tandem rig if you are not certain which phase will be more important that evening. You can copy both hatches at the same time.

A word of caution when using the tandem: Often by the time you set the hook, the trout has struck and moved away from the fly. It is imperative that you set the hook immediately. How do you do this? Keep as tight a line as possible and strike quickly if your dry fly or other strike indicator moves. Make certain you mend the line to keep any loops or bends out of your line. The fewer arcs or bends in your line, the easier and quicker it is to set the hook. If trout continue to strike short, you might even want to try trailing a hook off your wet fly.

> **TIP**
>
> Some spinners die on the surface spent and later sink underneath. Often a spinner pattern tugged underneath works during a spinnerfall. Add weight to some of your Trico spinner patterns when you tie them, and fish them as the point (wet) fly in a tandem setup.

Montana's Kootenai River has good hatches of caddis and mayflies, but you can fool the trout with only a few patterns—as long as you fish them correctly.

Use a Wet Fly

I carry three basic wet flies with me at all times to use in a tandem rig, especially when trout refuse the dry fly: Beadhead Pheasant Tail, BLM, and the Zebra Midge.

"You don't go to the Metolius River in Oregon and try a new fly. They just don't take new flies. These trout have PhDs." That's what Kevin Mead said to Bryan Meck about one of Kevin's favorite, but sometimes frustrating, waters in the middle of an early April snow squall. The Metolius is pounded. Fishing pressure abounds on this fantastic, challenging, fertile water just a couple of hours south of Portland.

Jay Kapolka and I would have to agree with Kevin's assessment. We both fished this river 20 years ago and found the trout difficult to catch even when we encountered four separate hatches on the river at one time.

But more recently, Kevin and Bryan did catch fish while the other half a dozen anglers in the areas did not. Was it the fly-fishing skill? Was it the location? Was it the fly? Probably yes to all the questions! It was a new fly, one Kevin and Bryan had never used before. And the two of them caught eight trout in a couple of hours of fishing on a cold, blustery snow-flurry-laden day. Six other anglers fished nearby Bryan and Kevin, and in the two hours I watched they didn't catch anything. But Bryan and Kevin did.

At one point Kevin changed to a size 20 Little Blue-Winged Olive to fish over a trio of risers in an eddy. But by the time he tied on the dry fly the fish stopped rising.

What pattern did they use and why did it work? What set their fishing apart from the other highly skilled anglers? All eight fished while a fairly decent Little Blue-Winged Olive hatch appeared. Occasionally a trout would rise in a slow eddy for one of the laggards too cold to take flight. But Bryan and Kevin stuck to a wet fly—a size 20 wet fly. Why in the world would these educated green-back rainbows be taking that small wet fly? I am convinced that the wet fly called the BLM (Beaded Little Mayfly), created by Tim Heng, worked because it suggested to trout an emerging Little Blue-Winged Olive. Bryan once dropped the BLM in an eddy, and a nice rainbow chased it. That convinced me that that fish mistook it for a small mayfly emerger. Both fished the pattern near the bottom and both used a large strike indicator in this heavy, roaring river. And both caught trout—some nearly 20 inches long—on that measly size 20 wet fly.

The lesson we learned that day: Although these trout are difficult, they will take an appropriate fly fished at the appropriate depth. They do not have PhDs!

If you don't have any luck with your dry fly and you don't have any success twitching the dry fly or tug-

---

BLM

Hook:	#18-20 caddis
Bead:	Brass
Tail:	Green Angel Hair, three or four strands
Body:	Green Angel Hair, ribbed with fine copper wire

Note: There are many variations to this recipe.

---

ging it underneath, then try a wet fly like the BLM. If you're fishing a Sulphur or PMD hatch try a Beadhead Pheasant Tail. That latter nymph pattern copies those larvae adequately.

The more I fish the pattern and the more trout I see hit that fly, the more convinced I become that it copies some emergers like the Blue-Winged Olive. Try it!

Twitching your dry fly is a deadly technique on small streams. You don't want to move your fly so much that you spook the trout, but a little motion can suggest food to them.

If trout refuse your fly and you feel you have an adequate imitation, move your fly. Tug that fly underneath the surface if the normal floating fly doesn't work. Use a fly smaller than the hatch if you're casting on heavily fished waters. Or, if you see some cripples, add a shuck to your dry fly. And don't forget to use a BLM wet fly (or the Pheasant Tail with a Sulphur and PMD hatch) if you're fishing over a small mayfly hatch. All of these unorthodox techniques can catch trout during a hatch when nothing else seems to work. Combined, they make matching the hatches, and catching trout, much easier. All of these methods make up step 6 (fish multiple hatches) in your effort to catch more trout when a hatch appears.

Created in Arizona on the Lees Ferry section of the Colorado River by Edward (Ted) Welling, the Zebra Midge is my go-to

Zebra Midge

Hook:	#16-22 curved shank
Thread:	Black 6/0
Body:	Tying thread
Rib:	Fine silver wire
Bead:	Brass

fly when no hatch appears or fish are taking midges. This fly is truly a fishing-trip-saver and one I resort to often. The smaller the Zebra, the better your chances when fishing over heavily fished trout. My son, Bryan, has caught innumerable trout over 20 inches long on a size 20 or 22 Zebra Midge. If trout are midging near the surface, I tie the Zebra as a point fly six inches behind a large easy-to-see dry fly. If trout are taking midges, try this pattern.

Why is the Beadhead Pheasant Tail a top producer with or without a hatch? This productive pattern adequately copies many important mayfly nymphs like the PMD and Sulphur. Fish the pattern in the middle of a hatch and you'll catch trout. Fish the pattern when no hatch appears and you'll catch trout.

Beadhead Pheasant Tail

Hook:	#12-16 curved shank
Bead:	Brass
Thread:	Reddish brown 6/0
Tail:	Pheasant tail tips
Body:	Pheasant tail fibers
Rib:	Fine gold wire
Hackle:	Pheasant tail-tip fibers

Note: Add 6 to 8 wraps of .010 lead wire to the hook shank before you tie this fly and use the Beadhead Pheasant Tail as a dropper behind a dry fly.

Use Unconventional Flies

Not all hatches remain a pleasant memory for me. Some were total disasters because I wasn't prepared, like the first time I fished the Brown Drake hatch and spinnerfall on Pine Creek in north central Pennsylvania. Jim Heltzel and I stopped at the Cedar Run section on June 1 several decades ago, and within an hour we were engulfed in one of the thickest, heaviest, most concentrated dun hatches and spinnerfalls that I have ever experienced. As duns emerged on the water in front of us, last night's duns and tonight's spinners flew in a heavy swarm upstream to lay their eggs. So many spinners filled the evening air that you could actually hear the humming noise from their wings. The spinners fell—and

When you hit a hatch—and you have the right patterns—you could have the best fishing of your life.

99

Often, your best bet to catch fish that have seen a lot of flies is to fish something that they have never seen before.

quickly—and we grabbed March Browns to match the spinnerfall. In an instant, ten trout rose within casting range. In a few more minutes—by the time I had tied on the fly—30 more trout joined the feeding frenzy. Both of us began casting to rising trout. At first it looked like a quail hunt where you shoot indiscriminately at the covey. We did the same with the growing number of risers in front of us. We cast, then recast, and then cast again over dozens of rising trout and still no takers. Irritating refusals went on for a half hour that seemed liked hours until we decided to try another pattern—in the midst of a fantastic hatch that neither of us had expected or had prepared for. Next on our agenda was a size 12 Black Quill pattern. Finally after almost 45 minutes of barren fishing, I picked up a small brown. Jim also picked up a trout on his Black Quill fly. But strikes were few and far between, and we again grew frustrated with our lack of any real success; and yet hundreds of trout fed steadily on what seemed like an unending supply of Brown Drake spinners.

I almost hoped for the hatch and fall to end that evening—and thankfully it did about an hour or so after it had begun. I hoped for the end because the more that I fished that event, the more frustrated I became. Hatches unmatched cause total frustration. Finally the waters grew calm—few spinners remained on the surface and only an occasional trout took one of the large morsels. Thank God, the hatch and fall had ended.

On the 80-mile trip back home that evening, I went over what had happened and vowed I'd change my ways of fishing the hatches forever. That disastrous event occurred more than 35 years ago, but the memory still remains a vivid picture in my mind. Who says we tend to forget those unhappy experiences of the past?

One of the most difficult decisions a fly fisher has to contend with is pattern selection. The choice of patterns when fishing can be the ultimate determiner in whether or not you succeed. Choosing the right fly when matching a hatch is even more important. Would you like to match just about every hatch you'll ever encounter with just one fly? You heard me—one fly. In this chapter, we'll examine some methods to match every hatch you ever meet.

> **TIP**
>
> Dark duns have darker spinners; light duns have lighter spinners. Look at the Blue-Winged Olive as an example. The dun's body is usually an olive color whereas the spinner is dark olive, almost black. Cream Cahills turn into almost pure white spinners. A spinner carrying eggs has a different, often darker, color.

COLOR MATCHER FLIES

For the past 10 years, I have extensively fished a Chamois Leech pattern when there's no hatch. That particular fly is nothing more than a ⅛-inch-wide strip of chamois tied on a weighted hook. Most flies are about 2 to 3 inches long. I color the chamois a bright red with a permanent marking pen. That red color and chamois material really work well and the pattern catches a lot of trout when there's no hatch. And I can fish the red Chamois Leech for a couple hours before it loses its bright red color.

Why not try the same technique on a dry fly copying a hatch? That's something I've wanted to do since I began fly fishing. With the right tying material and the appropriate permanent marking pen colors, you can match any hatch on any stream with one basic fly. Permanent markers have evolved in the past few years. A decade or so ago the variety of colors available was limited. Now you can purchase just about any color you want and almost immediately copy any hatch. What effect does coloring the white Color Matcher fly have? So much for carrying a complete list of every possible hatch you think you'll encounter. No need to do that anymore. This is an especially important way to fish the hatches on a stream you've never fished before. How I wish I would have taken these flies and pens with me on my inaugural trip to New Zealand.

> **TIP**
>
> It's easier to make a pattern smaller on the water than it is to make it larger. Carry scissors with you on the stream to trim flies to exact size.

I'm not the first angler to think of this method of matching the hatches. Several years ago Mike Klimkos, editor of *Mid Atlantic Fly Fishing Guide*, wrote an article for the Cumberland Valley Trout Unlimited's booklet called *CVTU's Favorite Flies*. Mike titled his article (and the fly he recommended) "What Haven't I Dun?". Mike recommended a Catskill-type dry fly with white poly wings, white rabbit body, white hackle, and tail. He carried a dozen Sharpie permanent markers in all the important colors with him.

I also carry a wide variety of fine-tip permanent marking pens in an extensive assortment of colors. I use Bic pens, sold at Staples. They come in a vast array of colors—gray, brown, tan, orange, red, black, olive-green, pink, pale yellow, yellow, and many more. There are several shades of tan and gray. I also carry plenty of Color Matcher flies with white poly yarn wings, white tail, white stripped hackle body, and white hackle tied parachute style. Have them available in sizes 12 to 20. And don't forget to take down-wing patterns like the Color Matcher Caddis in sizes 12 to 18, all with white bodies and white poly yarn wings. Add a white hackle for a fluttering caddis. With a white-bodied fly and the pens in an assortment of colors, you can match just about any hatch you'll encounter. If the color isn't just right, experiment with a second color. Most caddisflies you'll encounter will have dark brown, gray, green, cream, or black bodies, so be sure to carry these colors with you. They are all nontoxic. In a completely unexpected situation or unknown hatch, you can copy the insect streamside almost immediately and very effectively. The intensity of the permanent pen's color will fade a bit after an hour of use. If it becomes too light just reapply the original color.

You can use old caddis patterns, wet or dry, and add a darker color with a pen. Recently, in early May, I hit a Grannom hatch and had no wet fly to match the almost-black body of the natural. I used a Tan Caddis pattern I found in my fly box and darkened it with a black permanent pen. For the next half hour I had 10 strikes on that pattern.

Scott Young and I hit a Blue-Winged Olive hatch on a mid-June afternoon recently. I suggested that he switch to an olive-bodied pattern to copy the hatch. The closest pattern he had with him was a size 14 Adams. I quickly got an olive-green permanent marker out of my pocket and began coloring the Adams. On the first cast with that hybrid fly he caught a trout. On the third cast he landed another trout. That recolored Adams really worked.

The Dark Brown dun on the Henry's Fork is another example. I had never heard nor seen this size 20 hatch before, and I wasn't prepared for it. Thousands and thousands of these tiny mayflies floated like a parade on the surface in front of me, and trout picked them off in ones, twos, and threes. I had no match. The closest thing I had was a Little Blue-Winged Olive, but I had only mediocre results with that. I waded to shore and got a dark brown

Color Matcher Dry Fly

Hook:	#12-20
Thread:	White
Tail:	White hackle fibers
Body:	Stripped white hackle stem
Wings:	White poly yarn (use white turkey if you plan to use dye)
Hackle:	White hackle

Color Matcher Wet Fly

Hook:	#12-20
Weight:	Lead wire (optional)
Thread:	White
Tail:	White hackle fibers
Body:	Stripped white hackle stem
Wings:	White hackle, tied down-wing
Hackle:	Two turns of white hen hackle

Note: The color fades after about an hour of use, and you might have to switch flies or use the same fly and color the faded fly again with a permanent marker.

Color Matcher Spinner

Hook: #12-20
Thread: White
Tail: White hackle fibers
Body: Stripped white hackle stem
Wings: White hackle

Color Matcher Caddis

Hook: #12-20
Thread: White
Body: White vernille about 1½ inches long
Wings: White poly yarn

Note: I sometimes use a ⅛-inch-wide or smaller strip of closed-cell packing sheet and wind that strip around the bend of the hook, but it can be difficult to color with a pen.

marking pen and a size 20 Color Matcher fly. I colored the body with the dark brown pen, the tail and legs cream, and the wings gray. That makeshift permanent-pen-marked fly worked that afternoon, and it has worked on many other occasions since.

Carry some pens and Color Matcher flies with you and you'll be prepared for even the lesser-known, unexpected hatches. Try this method if you plan to fish strange waters, especially where you have little access to fly shops. I prefer to tie parachute Color Matchers. This type of fly is easier to color. Often the color of the thorax of a mayfly or caddisfly is darker than the body. With marking pens, you can get that color. This coloring technique works especially well when you plan to fish a stream you've never fished before, including streams and rivers of New Zealand and Argentina and even Labrador.

But that's not the only way you can use Color Matcher flies. Add some medium gray to dark gray Rit dye to water, add a Color Matcher fly for a couple of minutes, and you have a pattern copying the ubiquitous Blue Quill. Add brown dye and a Color Matcher fly and you have an instant Western March Brown. Rinse the dyed fly under cold water and you have instant long-lasting color.

Color Matcher spinner patterns also work well. Take a look at the Blue-Winged Olive dun (*Drunella cornuta*) that appears in late May and early June. The color of the spinner body can be difficult to copy. Mark with a black pen, let the ink dry, and then add a covering of olive to get that elusive olive-black sheen you need for the spinner body. Add dark olive to the tail and you've got a killer pattern to fish when the Dark Olive spinner falls on many streams of the East and Midwest.

Summer also brings on some spinnerfalls that are practically all white, plus in late summer you'll see White Flies on many waters. The Color Matcher Spinner—with no added color—works well during these spinnerfalls.

The Color Matcher concept can also be applied to caddisflies and stoneflies. Just this past year, I purposely fished the Grannom on central Pennsylvania's Little Juniata River in April armed only with Color Matcher down-wings. I carried size 12, 14, and 16 down-wings and colored the bodies black streamside. Again, they worked exceptionally well.

1. Tie in your wingpost at midshank. You can use poly, Antron, or other material. Wrap your tying thread around the base of the wingpost to provide a firm, smooth surface around which to wrap the hackle.

2. Tie in a length of vernille at the base of the wingpost and wrap back to a point just before the bend of the hook. Leave the body long if you want to be able to trim and color it on the water.

3. Wrap your parachute hackle and tie it off. Leave the wingpost long if you want to be able to trim it to size on the water.

4. Use a marker to color the body to match the natural. I do this on stream, or at the vise if I know ahead of time the color of the insect that I want to match.

5. The colored fly.

6. Cut the body a length that matches the natural's body. For a more finished look, you can scorch the end of the vernille with a match or lighter.

7. The finished fly.

CONVERTIBLE FLIES

Craig Hull of Camp Hill is an active supporter of the Cumberland Valley Trout Unlimited in south central Pennsylvania and a terrifically innovative fly tier. Recently that premier organization held a workshop for new fly fishers. Craig was one of the instructors in that half-day program, and he demonstrated tying a convertible fly.

With his convertible pattern, Craig can reposition the wings and convert the fly from one copying an emerging dun resting on the surface to a spent-wing spinner. How does he do it? Look at the Red Quill he tied that day.

The classic Catskill-style dry fly is the perfect pattern to create a convertible fly. It is easily modified to represent a number of different mayfly species. It is easy to tie even though many people think winged patterns are difficult to construct. The wings are the key to this pattern and are also what makes the pattern the perfect choice for convertible flies. After Craig places the hook in the vise, he lays down a small base of tying thread about ⅛ to ³⁄₁₆ inch long just behind the eye. The thread is left in the center of this base of tying thread. Be certain that you leave enough room for the hackle and a tapered head. Next, Craig prepares two wood-duck (or imitation) feathers to create the wings. He removes the fuzz and short feather fibers from both sides of the stem. He also removes a short section of the center stem of both feathers. The feathers are now ready to start the process of making the wings.

TIP

To copy a spent caddis, spread the wings with your fingers on your down-wing pattern so the wings look spent.

Craig stacks the two feathers on top of each other with the convex sides up. The tips of the feathers are evenly aligned and held in the left hand facing to the right, while securely holding the stems and fibers at the appropriate length of the wings. He lays the tips of the feathers on the inside of the middle finger of the right hand. He then uses the index finger and thumb of the right hand to fold the feathers over and hold them tight. He maintains the left hand grip while placing the feathers at the bend to gauge the proper wing length. The tips should extend just beyond the eye of the hook. Readjust the position of the left hand to achieve the desired length of the wing.

The wing bundle is laid directly over the tying thread. Craig uses two pinched loops to secure the wing bundle directly on top of the hook and then adds several additional loops of thread to permanently secure the wing bundle in place. The feather butts are clipped off in a tapered fashion directly behind the tying thread. He uses additional wraps to completely cover the tapered butt section of the wing bundle. He leaves the wing bundle laying flat and extending forward over the eye of the hook. He then ties in the tail and the appropriate body of the mayfly he is imitating.

After he completes the body and tail, he stands the wing bundle upright and makes 10 to 12 wraps of tying thread in front of the bundle to maintain the upright position.

Craig's secret to separating the wings is what makes his approach to tying this pattern unique. Craig uses his right thumbnail to divide the wing into two equally divided wings. With backward and downward pressure of his right thumbnail, Craig pinches the bundle down over the hook shank. If the wing bundle was initially tied on top of the shank, the bundle will separate with equal amounts of the fiber on each side of the hook shank. The tip of the wing closer to the tier is held as several X wraps are made between the wings to maintain the separation.

Instead of using the figure eight technique to finish the wings, Craig posts each wing separately. Several loose wraps of the thread are placed at the base of each wing. The tip of the wing is held as those are pulled tight. Then several more wraps are added to crush the wing fibers together. This causes the tip the wing to flare out and makes a more natural looking mayfly wing. Place one wrap of the thread around the shank to secure the wing in place. Repeat the process with the other wing and finish the fly with the hackle and head.

Craig's approach not only makes the wings of a Catskill pattern easier, but they also look more realistic. An added benefit to his approach is that it allows the angler to flatten the wings out to the sides of the fly. If you

A Pale Morning Dun spinner appears on the surface unexpectedly on this small stream and all you have is a copy of a PMD. With a convertible pattern, you can change it from an upright one to a spent one in seconds.

remove the hackle from the bottom, the fly will float like a spinner. Within minutes, the fly is easily converted from a high-floating dun pattern to a spent spinner. Eliminating the figure eight when you tie the wings allows the wings to lie flat because they are not tied together.

Carry scissors with you, and if trout refuse your Catskill-type pattern, trim the hackle off the bottom so it floats more flush with the surface. This one simple technique often catches trout. Your scissors will also come in handy if you decide to try the Quick Trim flies.

THE QUICK TRIM FLY

The basic concept behind the Quick Trim series of flies, which includes duns, spinners, wet flies, and down-wings, is that you tie flies with larger bodies and wings than what you anticipate needing. Carry these generic patterns with you on the water, and trim them on the spot to match the naturals that you observe. Combine this with the Color Matcher concept, and with a couple of cuts and a marking pen, you have a match for almost any hatch.

I tie the Quick Trim flies with two different body types, vernille and white foam. If you use thin white foam (2 mm) or a strip of closed-cell packing sheet, cut it about 1/8-inch wide. (It's difficult to color the strips of the packing sheet with a permanent marker.)

Quick Trim Fly

Hook:	#16-20 dry fly
Thread:	White
Body:	Very fine white vernille or thin white foam extended well beyond the bend
Wings:	Very long white or pale gray poly yarn, tied parachute style
Hackle:	Cream hackle (for #12-14 fly)

Note: Color the vernille body the appropriate color with a permanent marker. The body is about 1 1/2 inches long, so you can conceivably copy large drakes.

Quick Trim Spinner

Hook:	#16-20 dry fly
Thread:	White
Body:	Very fine white vernille or thin white foam extended well beyond the bend
Wings:	Very long white or gray poly yarn

Note: Color the vernille body the appropriate color with a permanent marker. The body is about 1 1/2 inches long, so you can conceivably copy large spent spinners.

For most of my mayfly patterns, I tie in a body that is about 1½ inches long and wings that are appropriate for a size 8, 10, or 12 fly. If a Yellow Drake appears, you're set with the correct size. Just color the body, legs, and wings a pale yellow with your permanent marking pen. I tie parachute-type wings with a post, but, if you prefer, you can split the wings. Remember, you want the body and wings about the length of a size 10 fly pattern. If a size 12 or 14 Light Cahill appears that evening, trim off part of the body and the wings commensurate with a pattern that size. If you hit a size 16 Sulphur, start trimming again. Cut a chunk off the end of the body so it more closely represents a size 16 Sulphur, and cut off part of the poly wing so it more readily copies a size 16 fly. If a size 18 Pale Evening Dun emerges, start cutting and trimming to match the

Quick Trim Wet Fly

Hook:	#16 wet fly
Thread:	White
Body:	Very fine white vernille extended well beyond the bend
Wings:	White hen hackle that extends well past the bend of the hook
Hackle:	Cream

Note: You can make the wet flies sink more quickly by adding a few wraps of .005 or .010 lead.

Quick Trim Caddis

Hook:	#16 dry fly
Thread:	White
Body:	White vernille or thin white foam cut in ⅛-inch strips
Wings:	White poly yarn
Legs:	White or cream hackle

size of the natural. Now you're set. Without removing the fly from the tippet and within a few seconds, you can match a smaller hatch with a Quick Trim fly.

To match even smaller hatches, tie smaller Quick Trim flies on a size 20 dry-fly hook and tie in a ½-inch piece of vernille. Make the post about ½-inch long. With this smaller Quick Trim fly, you can match most of the smaller hatches like olives, Tricos, and Blue Duns in sizes 18 to 24.

No matter what size the hatch, with a few cuts of the wings and the body, you can match many sizes. And you can color the white body any color to match the hatch. So in a few seconds you can color the body and wings and trim the body and wings to copy almost any hatch.

With a good selection of Color Matcher and Quick Trim flies, and an assortment of permanent markers, you will be prepared to match any mayfly hatch. Experiment with your own designs and colors to match local hatches.

My frustrating encounter with the Brown Drakes occurred more than 30 years ago. What would have happened if I had a Quick Trim fly with me? In seconds I could have colored the wings brown and the body and legs tannish brown. I could have left the body as long as the dun I had captured so I could have been certain about the size of the artificial. By comparing it with a nearby natural, that whole evening might have turned out differently.

Observe Nature

N ature can affect the hatches immensely. With a limited knowledge of some of the more common flowers and when they bloom, you can make matching the hatches much easier. And if you realize that some hatches seem to appear on some of the worst weather days, you can be forewarned that you just might experience the hatch of a lifetime.

Diverse conditions like temperature, precipitation, vegetation, and time of year—all affect and predict the emergence time and most likely the color of many of the hatches. And all can help determine whether or not you will experience a memorable or frustrating day. It's difficult to remember all the hatches and when they appear; and don't forget, hatches can vary

Paul Weamer stalks a rising trout on Pennsylvania's Spring Creek.

by as much as a month from year to year because of location and weather. By comparing a few flowers with some of the major hatches, you'll likely hit these hatches more often.

But as much as you'd like to you often can't plan your life around inclement days. Don't we just go fishing when we have an opportunity? With some knowledge about what affects the hatches and how, you might not have to cancel that next trip on a lousy day. Let me explain.

Insects emerge at the same time that certain flowers bloom. By noting these coincidences, you can predict when major hatches will occur in your area.

Just recently I scheduled a fishing trip for a Saturday. It drizzled that morning, and the air temperature never rose above 45 degrees. My friend cancelled on me, but I decided to go because of the convergence of conditions. Little Blue-Winged Olives didn't disappoint me—they emerged in that cold environment for more than two hours. And trout rose under those conditions.

Inclement days can also create some unusual situations if a hatch appears. Too much rainfall might shut down the hatch completely—if a fine drizzle falls, however, you might experience the hatch of a lifetime.

Weather affects both plants and animals and that includes insects like mayflies. We explore these diverse conditions and more in this chapter. Nature is important and interactive and a more thorough understanding of these interactions will help you match the hatch and catch more trout.

MATCH THAT FLOWER—PHENOLOGY

Wow! What a spring 2010 turned out to be. In late March the Northeast experienced several days near 90 degrees. All of the early hatches, those appearing normally in April, appeared in March and early April. What a great argument for year-round fly fishing! This goes for all states. The Little Blue-Winged Olive hatched in great numbers on March 10 on central Pennsylvania's Big Fishing Creek; the Hendrickson in the same general vicinity emerged in late March and the first couple days in April. The official trout season for that area of Pennsylvania began on April 17, well after all the spring hatches had ended. Why not stock marginal streams in the fall, allow fishing over these trout until the next April, and then allow keeping trout? That way fly fishers wouldn't miss any of the early hatches brought on by unusually warm conditions.

Also in the spring of 2010 vegetation appeared early. Forsythias bloomed in late March in central Pennsylvania. Apple trees bloomed in mid-April, redbuds in mid-April, and lilacs on April 25. For years I equated the blooming of the lilac with the initial appearance of the Sulphur: 2010 was an excellent time to test my theory. In a normal year in central Pennsylvania, the Sulphur appears around May 8 and the lilac blooms about the same date. In 2010 the lilac bloomed on April 25 and guess what? The Sulphur first appeared that same date. Scientists call this comparison phenology.

Phenology is defined as a branch of science dealing with the relationship between climate and periodic biological phenomena such as bird migration or plant flowering. I first recognized that flowers blooming at the time certain hatches appeared occurred with regularity year after year more than 40 years ago. I wrote about this phenomenon in *Meeting and Fishing the Hatches* in 1977: "Nature works in orderly ways. As the forsythia begins blooming in late April in central Pennsylvania, so then does the Hendrickson begin its annual appearance. When the locust tree is full of fragrant, white blossoms, the Green Drake is leaving its muddy aquatic habitat and emerging on the surface. Many plants and animals, including mayflies, caddisflies, and stoneflies, appear with some scheduled regularity year after year."

What really reinforced this matching-the-flower-with-a-hatch-that's-emerging business was my lengthy experience with the Brown Drake hatch. The Brown Drake (*Ephemera simulans*) is one of a handful of mayflies that is ubiquitous—it appears in the Eastern, Midwestern, and Western United States. It even appears on brook trout waters in Labrador. The Eastern hatch often appears near the end of May. For years I've equated the hatch with the blooming of the commercial rhododendron—usually purple in color. For decades I've noted that when the rhododendron in my

> **TIP**
>
> On warm days hatches start earlier. Hendricksons can appear as early as 9 a.m., and Brown Drakes hatch even earlier. See Hendricksons in chapter 8 on page 130.

BUGS AND BLOOMS

Insect	Location	Hatch Date	Flower
Big Slate Drake (Hexagenia atrocaudata)	E, M	8/15	Goldenrod blooming; mullein opening
Black Quill (Leptophlebia cupida)	E, M	4/20	Redbud bright; dandelion blooming
Blue Quill (Paraleptophlebia adoptiva)	E, M	4/6	Forsythia heavily budded; marsh marigold blooming
Blue Quill, Mahogany dun (Paraleptophlebia memorialis)	W	5/15–7/15	Lilac open
Blue-Winged Olive dun (Drunella cornuta)	E, M	5/25	Oxeye daisy opening; peony open, iris open
Brown Drake (Ephemera simulans)	All	5/28	Domestic rhododendron blooming
Dark Quill Gordon (Ameletus ludens)	E, M	4/15	Forsythia opening
Golden Drake (Anthopotamus distinctus)	E, M	6/20	Elderberry open
Green Drake (Ephemera guttulata)	E	5/27	Locust tree blooming; horse chestnut blooming
Hendrickson (Ephemerella subvaria)	E, M	4/29–4/25	Forsythia opening
Light Cahill (Stenacron interpunctatum)	E, M	5/25	Oxeye daisy opening
Little Blue-Winged Olive Dun (Baetis tricaudatus)	All	3/25	Coltsfoot
Little Blue-Winged Olive Dun (second generation)	All	9/1	White snakeroot blooming

Phenology is matching flower bloom dates with the hatches. Since *Meeting and Fishing the Hatches* was published, and my experience with the Brown Drake, I have noted dozens of other flowers that commonly occur when a hatch appears. I have noted those appearing year after year in the table above. Emergence dates for aquatic insects can vary considerably from year to year even on the same stream. They can vary as much as a couple of weeks or more. But by watching the flower blooms you will be able to stay in tune with these hatches.

BUGS AND BLOOMS continued

Insect	Location	Hatch Date	Flower
March Brown (*Maccaffertium vicarium*)	E, M	5/15	Dame's rocket blooming
Pale Evening Dun (*Ephemerella dorothea dorothea*)	E, M	6/1	Mountain laurel blooming
Pale Morning Dun (*Ephemerella excrucians*)	W	5/20–7/25	Lilac blooming
Quill Gordon (*Epeorus pleuralis*)	E	4/8–4/25	Forsythia heavily budded with a few open flowers
Salmonfly (*Pteronarcys californica*)	W	5/20–7/15	Lilac past full bloom
Slate Drake (*Isonychia bicolor*)	E, M	5/25	Oxeye daisy opening
Slate Drake (second generation)	E, M	9/10	White snakeroot blooming
Sulphur (*Ephemerella invaria*)	E, M	5/7	Lilac blooming; apple blossoms
Summer Blue Quill (*Paraleptophlebia guttata*)	E, M	6/15	Chicory blooming; tiger lily blooming
Trico (*Tricorythodes* spp.)	All	7/15–10/15	Spotted knapweed open; mullein just opening
Western Green Drake (*Drunella grandis grandis*)	W	5/20–7/10	Oxeye daisy just open; some petals on locust tree are falling
White Fly (*Ephoron leukon, E. album*)	All	8/15–9/10	New England aster opening
Western March Brown (*Rhithrogena morrisoni*)	W	2/25–5/1	Daffodil open, forsythia just about open, magnolia blooming, flowering plum open, dandelion open
Yellow Drake (*Ephemera varia*)	E, M	6/13	Chicory blooming; elderberry ready to open

front yard bloomed, then the Brown Drake emerged locally. A decade or so ago I fished the famed Henry's Fork in Idaho near the end of June. I fished the stretch near the Box Canyon area. For the past three evenings I had fished the same river, only several miles downstream, and each night—at dusk—I hit a fabulous Brown Drake hatch. As I hiked back in the dark my flashlight shined on a rhododendron blooming in the ranger's yard— exactly when the Brown Drake appeared on Henry's Fork. That incident, followed by many more instances, reaffirmed my conviction and belief in phenology. The Brown Drake emerged in the Midwest in early to mid June, depending on the location. That's the same time the rhododendron is in full bloom in that area.

Emergence dates for aquatic insects can vary considerably from year to year even on the same stream. They can vary as much as a couple of weeks or more. Earlier I said I saw Sulphurs emerge as early as April 25 on the Little Juniata River in central Pennsylvania. Other cooler years I've noted the hatch beginning as late as May 12. Why? Cooler temperatures and less sunlight delay the hatch. The same goes for the blooming of flowers. Cooler-than-normal temperatures and less light can delay these flowers by a week or more. So doesn't it make sense that both the mayfly emergence and vegetation growth are regulated to some extent by weather? I said earlier that hatches in the West could vary from location to location by a month or more. Look at the Western Green Drake as a forceful example. I've seen hatches on the Metolius River in Oregon as early as late May and in late June and early July on the Bitterroot River in Montana and Henry's Fork in Idaho. Talk about variation. I've witnessed that same Green Drake hatch on the Frying Pan River just below the bottom-release Ruedi Reservoir in early September. The Pale Morning Dun also varies tremendously in the West. Hatches on Montana's Kootenai River often appear near the end of June; whereas on coastal and near coastal waters you'll often find the hatch a month earlier.

> **TIP**
>
> Watch the forecast. Heavy rain can delay or destroy a spinnerfall. I can't count the number of times that I've been rained out during a Trico spinnerfall, when I saw Tricos in the air and a sudden rainstorm came along and the Tricos disappeared.

Since *Meeting and Fishing the Hatches* was published, and my experience with the Brown Drake, I have noted dozens of other flowers that com-

René Harrop selects a fly from his box on the banks of the Henry's Fork of the Snake in Idaho. If you don't have the flowers in your area that are listed on the chart, keep your own journal of bugs and blooms.

monly occur when a hatch appears. I have noted those appearing year after year in the table on matching flowers with the hatches on page 116.

And believe it or not, many of the same flowers bloom in the West that are found in the East. For example around the Libby in Montana you find the mullein plant. It's a hairy wide-leafed plant that has yellow elongated clusters of flowers. The flowers first open two weeks later in northwestern

Hatches are often best on inclement days. Not only are hatches heavier, and insects often ride the water's surface for a longer period of time, trout feed with less caution in the low light.

Montana than they do in central Pennsylvania. The same goes for spotted knapweed found along Fisher River in northwestern Montana. It first blooms two weeks or more later than in central Pennsylvania. I equate the opening of the mullein and the spotted knapweed with the beginning of the Trico hatch in both regions.

Maybe only a few or none of the flowers listed in the table on page 116 grow in your area. How can you use phenology for your trout fishing? Keep a record of every fishing trip you take. Record the hatches you've encountered and the flowers blooming at the time of the hatch. You can refine your findings each year. I've kept a record of every fishing trip since 1968. That's more than 40 years of comparing hatches and flowers. By doing this you can have your own phenologic record and you'll be much better prepared to meet the hatches.

FISHING HATCHES ON INCLEMENT DAYS

What type of day is better to fish the hatches—a cloudy, cool day or a blue-bird day? Some of my worst matching-the-hatch days have occurred on those bright sunny days when the hatches escape rapidly. More times than I can remember, I have hit a spectacular Hendrickson hatch on a cloudy overcast day. The next day I fish the same hatch, but the weather clears and the hatch, although present, isn't nearly as productive as it was the day before.

Anything that delays a hatch from taking flight is a boon to the fly fisher. Those "anythings" include cold weather, a light rain or drizzle, cloudy conditions, and the right species of mayflies. Look for inclement days— plan for those days. Cool, inclement weather can enhance and lengthen a hatch. Try fishing rapidly escaping, sporadic hatches on inclement days.

Too much rain, however, can be a washout. Some species are normally slower to escape the surface than others. Even small species like the Dark Brown Dun (*Diphetor hageni*) will blanket the surface of some Western waters on warm days in July.

The boon to many anglers is a delayed flight—that is, a delayed flight of mayflies taking off. When the insects on the water's surface can't take flight immediately, they invite trout to feed on the surface. Things like a light drizzle and cool, cloudy weather affect the normal process of mayflies escaping. Mayflies must dry their wings—and drizzle and cold weather delay that. Many of the very best fishing days of my life occurred with lousy weather conditions when I fished over trout rising to an unending supply of insects for hours. In most instances with the lousy weather I never saw one other fly fisher. And that just didn't happen once—it has occurred many times over the past 30 years all over the United States. So if you want to fish the hatches and experience less-crowded stream conditions, then search out those inclement days and enjoy.

It was pure serendipity the first time I fished a Blue-Winged Olive hatch on July 4, 1979. I fished that day on central Pennsylvania's Penns Creek when thousands and thousands of Blue-Winged Olives struggled to free themselves from the cool drizzly surface and escape to nearby trees. That day only a very few mayflies did escape from the surface. Literally hundreds of hungry trout readily ate thousands

> **TIP**
>
> Scan the treetops for male mayfly spinners appearing before a major spinnerfall. Male spinners like the Brown Drake and the Coffin Fly (Green Drake) become active an hour or so before the spinners fall. Look for these large mayflies undulating near treetops along the stream.

DREARY DAY HATCHES

Hatch	Size	Scientific Name	Time of Day	Time of Year	Location
Blue Quill	#18	*Paraleptophlebia adoptiva*	M, A	4/1– 5/31	E, M
Blue Quill	#18	*Paraleptophlebia guttata*	M, A	6/1–8/31	E, M
Blue Quill	#18	*Paraleptophlebia memorialis*	M	5/1–7/31	W
Blue-Winged Olive Dun	#20	*Baetis intercalaris*	M, A	Year-round	W
Blue-Winged Olive Dun	#20	*Baetis tricaudatus*	M, A	Year-round	E, M, W
Blue-Winged Olive Dun	#14	*Drunella cornuta*	M, A	6/1–7/31	E, M
Blue-Winged Olive Dun	#14	*Drunella flavilinea*	M, E	5/1–7/31	W
Blue-Winged Olive Dun	#16	*Drunella lata*	M, A	7/1–8/1	E, M
Dark Blue Quill	#18-20	*Teloganopsis deficiens*	A	6/1–6/30	E, M
Hendrickson	#14	*Ephemerella subvaria*	A	4/1–5/31	E, M
Olive Sulphur (female) Dark Brown Dun (male)	#16	*Ephemerella needhami*	A, E	6/1–6/30	E
Pale Morning Dun	#16	*Ephemerella excrucians*	M, E	5/1–8/31	W
Pale Morning Dun	#16	*Ephemerella excrucians*	M, A, E	5/31–7/31	W
Quill Gordon	#14	*Epeorus pleuralis*	A	4/1–5/31	E
Sulphur	#16	*Ephemerella invaria*	A, E	5/1–6/30	E, M
Western Green Drake	#12	*Drunella grandis grandis*	M, A	5/1–7/31	W
Western March Brown	#14	*Rhithrogena morrisoni*	M, A	3/1–5/30	W

Cool, inclement weather can enhance and lengthen a hatch. Hot weather can accelerate the hatch. Blue-Winged Olives are perhaps the most famous insects that love cool, rainy weather.

of these dazed olive duns. Why not? These midseason mayflies were easy pickings. That episode reminded me of a hatchery at feeding time. Trout lost all timidity and fed wildly on the manna from heaven. I fished that day for six uninterrupted hours in a fine, cool drizzle and never saw one other

Inclement weather not only means good hatches and feeding fish, but it also means solitude on the water. Most people would rather stay indoors.

angler on the stream. I was certain that I was the only angler who had experienced this frenzied feeding on an inclement day. Why would a fly fisher in his or her right mind spend a midsummer day on an isolated stream under these miserable weather conditions? Why would anyone spend a day on the stream when the daytime high temperature never rose above 60 degrees and a slight drizzle fell much of the daylight hours?

In 1989 in *Pennsylvania Trout Streams and Their Hatches*, I wrote about that incident on Penns Creek. I explained how that day had become one of the greatest fishing events of my life. Within two months after the book was published, I received a letter from Andrew Leitzinger. He wrote:

> On July 4, 1979, in the late morning after a cold rain, I fished the upper no-kill stretch of Penns Creek from the Broadwaters to the Upper Island. I found the surface covered with Blue-Winged Olive mayflies. I fished this stretch and hooked and released 30 trout between 10 and 17 inches long. I missed many, many more. The water surface was quite broken as far as you could see with feeding fish.

I fished that day in complete solitude (I thought). I was cold, happy, and alone. I can remember how my shoulders ached from so many hours, and my thumb had become tattered by the teeth of the many trout that I had released. I stopped fishing at about 5:00 p.m. because I had reached a state just short of exhaustion. I exalted the cold gray heavens above me and gave thanks for a wonderful and unique gift.

So when I read your book and came across the passage on your experience at Penns Creek, I wondered what the odds were that such conditions had occurred more than once on a fourth of July in the past 10 years; a cold, light rain, a great hatch of Blue-Winged Olives, and a nearly deserted stream. If our two days were separate in time, then a statistical phenomenon has occurred to be noted! But if, as I hope, those two days were one and the same, then I am glad to know that one other person was able to share the exhilaration I felt that day. Those days, when all things come together, are few and far between and should never be taken for granted.

What an endorsement for lousy day fly fishing. That day on Penns Creek was the very best matching-the-hatch day that I've experienced in more than 50 years of angling. But there were others and in all areas of the country—some almost, but not quite, with the intensity of that Blue-Winged Olive.

Lousy fishing weather can also produce great memories in the West. Fishing on one of those lousy days on the Kootenai in northwestern Montana stands out as another highly productive day of matching the hatches. Other similar lousy-day-fishing events occurred on the Bitterroot River in Montana, Henry's Fork in Idaho, the Metolius and McKenzie rivers in Oregon, and the Animas in Colorado.

Take for instance the day Jay Kapolka and I fished the Metolius River in Oregon in late May of 1992. Jay and I fished the river below Sherman's Camp one day and suffered a surprisingly unproductive day on a normally great trout stream—I think each one of us caught a couple of trout in an afternoon of fishing. On our way back to Portland several days later, we decided to hit this same river again. I didn't want Jay to remember this fine river with one day of poor fishing.

Other events developed on that second trip: We hit a fine drizzle and the temperature hovered in the mid-fifties all day long. We almost decided to skip that day of fishing, but something told me to check the river on this lousy day. When we approached the fast-flowing water, we saw dozens of Metolius rainbows sipping dazed duns in an eddy in front of us. In that same whirling, slow stretch, we quickly noted hundreds of insects lying half dead on the surface too dazed and too cold to take flight. At least four separate species floated in that eddy on that blustery day—Little Blue-Winged Olives, Blue-Winged Olives, Green Drakes, and Pale Morning Duns—and all vied for the attention of more than a dozen feeding trout. We both selected the largest fly, the Green Drake, for a match and ended the day fishing a Blue-Winged Olive pattern. What a day of matching the hatches! Jay and I left that river that day convinced more than ever about the effects of a lousy day on fly fishing and how productive this river can be.

Well-known, well-publicized hatches produce more fishing pressure than normal. But inclement days with cooler temperatures and precipitation keep some—make that many—fly fishers off the stream.

The experience on the Metolius River wasn't an aberration—many others have occurred in the West. In chapter 1 I mentioned another memorable trip that occurred on one of those lousy days and a hatch of Western Green Drakes on the Bitterroot River near Missoula, Montana, on a late June day. A cool, overcast, drizzly day prevented those large dark olive mayflies from taking flight and trout fed for hours in the middle of the day.

In late June, my brother Jerry accompanied me on a trip to northwestern Montana and the Kootenai River above Libby. I've experienced some poor-to-fair days of fishing on the Kootenai, but weather that slows up the Pale Morning Dun hatch can bring the river alive. We had scheduled a float trip below the dam with Pennsylvania native Dave Blackburn. Even though we

> **TIP**
>
> Cool, inclement weather can enhance and lengthen a hatch. Hot weather can accelerate the hatch.

were greeted on this early July morning with a fine drizzle and cool air temperatures, we decided to head out on the downriver float. It didn't take long to reward us on that lousy day. PMDs, unable to take flight, rode the surface almost continuously for more than six hours. That hatch lasted all day long, and we caught dozens of trout on a size 16 PMD. That was the most memorable day of fishing a PMD hatch that I ever experienced.

One of the best fly-fishing events again occurred on an inclement day in central Pennsylvania in 2000 with a premature hatch of Sulphurs in mid-May. Often the first couple of days the Sulphur appears it does so during the afternoon. Add a lousy weather day to the equation and you might experience a spectacular, eventful day. For more than four hours Sulphurs emerged, rested, and trout fed on them—in the middle of the day.

Then there was the event in central Pennsylvania's Big Fishing Creek in April with a double hatch. Those hatches continued for more than four hours. And trout rose consistently throughout the extended hatch. First thousands of Little Blue-Winged Olives paraded in front of us, and wild trout picked off many that rode the surface for hundreds of feet in front of us. A cool drizzly afternoon slowed just about all the mayflies from taking flight. And we caught trout—plenty of trout—on a size 20 Little Blue-Winged Olive. About halfway through the hatch, trout began to refuse our pattern. But the hatch was as heavy as ever. After a frustrating half hour void of catching any trout, I finally examined one of the dazed mayflies on the surface. Now I knew why trout began refusing the Little Blue-Winged Olive. The fly in my hand was a Blue Quill. The Little Blue-Winged Olives had ended and a Blue Quill hatch had begun.

> **TIP**
>
> Check the water temperature of the stream you plan to fly-fish. That's as important early in the season as it is in the middle of a heat wave. Why? First, few insects appear if water temperatures are much below 45 degrees. In the past 50 years I've encountered several spectacular hatches in colder water. But trout feeding at the surface on this hatch is another story.

Hatches equal angling crowds. Add a Sulphur hatch to the Little Juniata River or Spring Creek in central Pennsylvania and you'll be searching for an area to fish. Add a Green Drake hatch to Penns Creek in the same area and again you'll see more fishing pressure. And the West is no different. The Frying Pan River in central Colorado comes alive with anglers when the Green Drake appears there. Michigan's Au Sable hosts plenty of anglers during the Slate Drake, Brown Drake, and Hex hatches. But add an inclement day to the equation and trout waters don't hold nearly the number of anglers as on a fair day.

But not all lousy days are productive. Take for instance that late September day Brad Waltman, Ty Churchwell, Dale Smith, and I fished the Animas River within the Durango city limits. Ty fishes the river more than a hundred times a year. He's also the backcountry coordinator for Trout Unlimited. Dale is a retired teacher and now guides on the Animas and other local rivers. Brad guided for years at Jackson Hole in Wyoming and has been fishing the rivers of southwestern Colorado for more than a decade. What a fantastic, well-informed trio to show me this excellent trout water.

When we arrived at 9 a.m. it began raining and continued throughout the morning. Not just a light rain, but a fairly heavy one. Now I said that Ty fishes this river almost 100 days a year and knows every rapids and pool in almost 100 miles of this productive river. He took us to an easy area to access, for me especially, right in the town. It continued to rain throughout the morning and by noon it poured. Throughout the morning a sporadic tiny Blue-Winged Olive Dun hatch appeared and trout responded by rising frequently. By 1 p.m. the river began to color a great deal, and trout seemed to sense that the river was getting darker and rose more often. Dozens of trout rose for Little Blue-Winged emergers just beneath the surface. They also sensed that the rain would soon darken the river too much for them to see. By 2 p.m. the trout shut off completely. Remember that: Too heavy a rain often cuts the hatch short. Although the hatch continued in lighter terms, the heavy rain unquestionably shortened the surface feeding activity. And by

Guide Mike Heck searches for rising trout on a foggy stretch of Letort Spring Run in Carlisle, Pennsylvania. Fish are more active in low light.

2 p.m. the chocolate-colored Animas was void of any rising trout. Too heavy a rain will shut off the hatch and also make the stream unfishable.

Ty says that the Little Blue-Winged Olive Dun hatch can produce fantastic hatches and many rises. Lousy days—not too severe mind you—will magnify the productivity of this fine trout river.

Mayflies need to dry their wings before they take flight, and this takes longer during cool or wet weather. This means that they ride on the surface for a longer period of time, encouraging trout to feed on them. Conversely, in sunny, hot weather, they leave the water quickly, making it more challenging for the fish.

So, too much rain can shut off a hatch or discolor the stream and shut down feeding. The ideal conditions are a cool air temperature, a fairly warm water temperature (50 to 65), very light rain or drizzle, a fairly clear trout stream, and of course a hatch appearing.

Some hatches seem to appear more on foul weather days than others. The hatch chart on page 122 shows some of the most productive hatches to match when lousy days appear. The king of lousy-day hatches has got to be the Little Blue-winged Olive dun. Show me a day of inclement weather and I'll show you Little Blue-Wings appearing. First, this hatch is very common from the East Coast to the West Coast. Second, a generous number of *Baetis* species can be copied by this one pattern. Third, the common species (*Baetis tricaudatus*) has a spring and fall generation.

There's another point to consider when fishing Western rivers in spring and early summer: That's when snowmelt occurs on these waters. I'll never forget the Bitterroot River in Montana when I first fished it on June 25 two decades ago. At the time it was running high from snowmelt still emanating from the nearby mountains. It was difficult to fish the Western Green Drake because of the high water. When I returned to the same spot on the same river three weeks later, the river was noticeably lower in level. So snowmelt can affect your fishing the hatches on Western waters. Snowmelt ends on northern Arizona streams by the end of April, in southern Colorado it ends in mid-June, and in Montana and Wyoming snowmelt usually has ended by mid-July.

TIME OF DAY THE HATCH APPEARS

Hatches often occur at the most comfortable time of the day. In early spring that most comfortable time is early afternoon. Examine the hatches in spring and most if not all appear on the surface from 11 a.m. to 4 p.m. Look at the Western March Brown of the coastal and near-coastal West. These mayflies appear daily from late February until May on the McKenzie of Oregon around 2 p.m. The Quill Gordon and Hendrickson in the East and Midwest appear usually from 1 p.m. to 3 p.m. Of course weather affects what time hatches appear.

In midsummer that most comfortable time is early morning and evening. Mayflies again tend to follow that general rule. In early spring and in fall hatches appear in the afternoon. In the summer most often hatches appear in early morning and late evening. In midsummer, Tricos and Blue Quills emerge as early as 6 a.m. (male Tricos even earlier), and others like

Fly fishers should strive to be as in tune with the natural world as their quarry.

some of the large Hex hatches appear at dark. Hatches in the spring and fall usually end by 4 or 5 p.m.

How is this useful to the angler? If you want to fish the hatches, then try to fish those most comfortable times of day. Your chances of meeting a hatch are much higher if you do. Weather variations like unusually hot weather, cold temperatures, rain, and other conditions can affect hatches tremendously. I've seen Brown Drakes in the early morning hours on hot days on Pine Creek in north central Pennsylvania. I've noted Hendricksons emerging at 9 a.m. on hot early spring mornings.

Seek the Dependable Hatches

ot all hatches are created equal. Some are better to fish than others. But no matter how good a hatch is, you must be on the right stream at the right time, with an adequate match. In other words, you've got to locate a hatch on a specific stream. And that's not all: if you fish one of the better-known streams, you often have to contend with angling crowds. Ask any angler who has ever fished the Green Drake hatch on central Pennsylvania's Penns Creek or any fly fisher on Michigan's Au Sable during the Hex, Slate Drake, or Brown Drake hatches. Even the diminutive Trico on Montana's Missouri River brings anglers out in great numbers. In this chapter I rate many of the major hatches. In chapter 10 you'll find some streams and rivers that hold those hatches.

Paul Weamer fishes on the Little Juniata River, a bug factory that has dependable hatches as long as weather and water levels do not fluctuate too much.

A hatch can be important on one stream and not on another. Look at three highly productive limestone streams: Penns Creek, Big Fishing Creek, and the lower Bald Eagle Creek, all in central Pennsylvania. Penns holds the mother of all Green Drake hatches; Big Fishing Creek boasts a smaller Green Drake in size and volume; and the lower Bald Eagle has nary a Green Drake. Why this variability in three streams in close proximity, all of which are fairly large and fairly cool? Why does one stream hold a hatch and another nearby stream not hold the same hatch? Chemical makeup of the stream has a lot to do with it.

> **TIP**
>
> A small mayfly that is found in all areas of the United States is the Little Blue-Winged Olive Dun (*Baetis tricaudatus*). Little Blue-Winged Olives can appear almost any day of the year.

Another top-notch nearby trout stream, the Little Juniata River, flows less than 50 miles away from all three. It has intermittently held Green Drake hatches for almost 30 years. Each time the hatch grew heavier on the Little J. Pollution, however, has entered the picture, and the hatch has disappeared.

One of the lower Bald Eagle's main tributaries is Spring Creek. During the summer months, Spring Creek makes up about three-quarters of the flow in the lower Bald Eagle. Spring lost its Green Drake hatch in 1957. Until that time, the hatch was dependable and heavy on that stream. That year a slug of chemicals entered the stream, and the Green Drake never reappeared. Pollution and sedimentation are two of the main negatives in the makeup of the hatches. Some hatches are more pollution resistant than others. The Sulphur seems to be one of the first to reappear on once-polluted waters.

To produce a memorable hatch-matching episode, you have to experience a number of events occurring or falling into place at one time. First, you must experience a hatch of insects. These insects can be aquatic or terrestrial. Aquatic insects include, but are not limited to, mayflies, stoneflies and caddisflies, and midges. Second, you must have an adequate match for the hatch. Rule 2 in chapter 2—be well prepared with a variety of patterns to copy the hatch—covers just that subject. Have you ever witnessed a hatch and you did not have the proper match? Next, if you want to fish a dry fly matching the hatch, you want a good number of these insects remaining on the surface as long as possible. Poor weather slows down the ascent of mayflies considerably. Poor weather includes a light rain or drizzle, cool weather, and overcast skies. There are many insects, however, that habitually remain on the surface for an extended period even under fair weather conditions. Many of these are large mayflies like the Green and Brown Drakes. It normally takes these bigger flies longer to become airborne.

Early season hatches—those appearing on cool days in March, April, and May, when they experience cool, overcast, drizzly days—can take forever to escape from the surface. On a warm day in early April, the Hendrickson escapes fairly quickly from the surface. If the same hatch experiences cool or inclement weather the next day, it might be a spectacular day to match the hatch.

Other mayflies, some fairly small, lie still on the surface for a few seconds or more. The diminutive Dark Brown Dun (*Diphetor hageni*) blankets Henry's Fork in early July. Trout seize these opportunities to feed voraciously on these tiny brown mayflies. The longer the mayfly rests on the surface, the more advantageous it is to the fly fisher, especially if he or she uses dry flies, and the more important it is to match the hatch.

It's wise to stock plenty of flies to match the most dependable hatches in your area. That way, you know you will be prepared for the most important insects.

THE MOST DEPENDABLE HATCHES

The Brown Drake is large, emerges in heavy concentrations, and is one of the few mayflies found in all three regions of the United States. Silver Creek and Henry's Fork in Idaho hold incredible Brown Drake hatches; the Au Sable in Michigan and the Delaware in New York and Pennsylvania also hold great hatches of this large dark brown mayfly. Labrador's Minipi River even boasts fantastic hatches. But meeting this large mayfly is often another story. It's a highly concentrated hatch, and on many waters this notable mayfly inhabits, mating ends a few days after it begins. Because the hatch and spinnerfall are so short-lived, it is often difficult to fish the hatch unless you schedule to be on the stream for a two-week period. If you ever hit this drake, it will probably be a momentous fishing event. For this reason, I rank it low in order of importance because the hatch is short-lived and difficult to time.

Conversely, look at the Summer Blue Quill, common on so many trout waters. Anglers often confuse this hatch with the Trico present on the waters at the same time. The Trico male spinners, however, move in a horizontal motion, and the Jenny Spinner, the male spinner of the Blue Quill, moves in a vertical motion. You'll see the Summer Blue Quill on many waters for three or four months.

But longevity does not always make a premier hatch. No matter how long this Blue Quill emerges, it usually does not rest on the surface any great time. The only times I've met this hatch with any success are on cool, overcast, drizzly early-summer mornings when the duns appear on the surface and can't take flight. Otherwise the hatch escapes too rapidly to be of any value to the dry-fly angler. Conversely, the early Blue Quill (*Paraleptophlebia adoptiva*) that appears in the East and Midwest in April usually encourages plenty of trout to feed on the surface because it typically remains on the surface for a while. So knowledge of the length of the hatch in days is of value to the angler if other aspects are in place. One of those other aspects that is important is whether the emerging duns or the falling spinners are available for any period for trout to feed on.

> **TIP**
>
> The longer the hatch appears in the season, the more selective trout become, especially on heavily fished streams.

Some hatches are sporadic and others concentrated. Sporadic hatches can appear for several hours each day for weeks but often in reduced numbers. Concentrated hatches often emerge for only an hour. When they

COMPARISON OF TOP HATCHES

Top Hatches	Best Overall	Most Overrated	Spinnerfall Is Important	Daytime Hatch
Black Quill				•
Blue Quill	•			•
Blue-Winged Olive Dun			•	•
Brown Drake	•		•	
Green Drake	•	•	•	
Hendrickson	•			•
Little Blue-Winged Olive				•
March Brown				•
Quill Gordon				•
Sulphur	•		•	•
Trico		•	•	•
Western Green Drake	•			•
Western March Brown	•			
White Fly	•		•	

Some hatches and spinnerfalls are more dependable than others. These five requisites make a hatch spectacular: a hatch that is *concentrated*; one that *lasts for a long period of the fishing season*; a hatch that is *fairly large* (size 18 hook or larger); and one that usually *rests on the surface* for an extended period. My top ten list appears on page 142 and include Sulphurs, Hendricksons, and Blue-Winged Olive Duns.

appear they often blanket the surface. The March Brown epitomizes sporadic emergences, and the Green Drake, Brown Drake, Sulphur, and dozens more represent concentrated ones.

Number of Days the Hatch Appears

Why should you know how long a hatch appears? How will this help you catch more trout? Compare a hatch with the daily feeding of trout at a hatchery. In a hatchery, trout feed voraciously on trout pellets. In the wild, trout do the same thing. But instead of pellets, it's insects. I've seen difficult trout lose their timidity completely and immediately when a hatch appears on the surface. The more days a specific hatch occurs in the year, the more

Western March Browns appear on the near-coastal McKenzie River in Oregon for 80 or more days. Fishing this hatch and many others with a boat is the best way to cover risers. Be prepared for this hatch from late March until mid-May in midafternoon.

important it is to be there when that hatch appears, armed with an appropriate pattern. What hatch appears for probably the most days of the year in the East and Midwest? Is it the Trico, the Little Blue-Winged Olive Dun, or the Slate Drake? Which hatches appear for a long time in the West? The Trico, Speckle-Winged Dun, and the Western March Brown each appear for more than a month.

In the Southwest you'll find Tricos appearing almost every day of the year. I've seen hatches on the Salt River near Phoenix, Arizona, on Christmas and New Year's mornings. The Little Blue-Winged Olive Dun also appears for many days on most Western waters. Fish the San Juan in New Mexico almost any day of the year and you're likely to see some Little Blue-Winged Olives appearing.

New Mexico's Red River north of Taos holds a good number of cuttbows that move upriver in late fall and early spring from the Rio Grande.

Manuel Monasterio, Bob Adams, Virgil Bradford, and I hiked into the Red River in mid-December a few years ago. Manuel at one time owned the Reel Life fly shops in Albuquerque and Santa Fe. It's extremely difficult getting into the lower end of the Red River. You have to descend a steep, rocky, narrow trail to reach the river below. Once we reached this 30-foot wide water we had other obstacles. Nature placed huge stones in our path as we hiked upriver. Boulders in the stream and along the bank protected each pool. Almost every cast was an effort to complete.

Around noon hundreds of Little Blue-Winged Olives appeared and a few trout fed on them. These mayflies appeared on a cold mid-December afternoon. Hatches of this species appear in good numbers on the Red River in March, April, September, and October. But trout did occasionally take one of these small olive mayflies on that cold day in December. The hike back up the steep hill to the car seemed to take hours to complete.

But many of the hatches and spinnerfalls that appear for 30 or more days also have a downside. Trout seem to become extremely selective on some of these after feeding on the hatch for a week or two. Fish the Sulphur on Spring Creek in central Pennsylvania in mid-May, if you can find a spot to fish, and you'll probably experience a great hatch-matching event. But come back a few weeks later and you might well encounter a different episode. In the many weeks that Tricos, Pale Morning Duns, or Sulphurs appear, trout see plenty of anglers and dozens of patterns on some of the more heavily fished streams. These trout become highly selective in the process.

Special situations create hatches that continue into the season for a longer period. Bottom-release dams and the tailwaters they create have an effect on hatching times. I mentioned the Western Green Drake in the Roaring Fork area earlier on page 39. That hatch first

> **TIP**
>
> Long-lasting sporadic hatches are often better to fish than concentrated ones that last only a short time.

begins around June 25 near Glenwood Springs and continues up Roaring Fork, then up the Frying Pan River, ending on that river in early September. The Sulphur on the Delaware River near Hancock, New York, is definitely affected by cool water from the bottom-release dams. Hatches continue throughout the summer in the daylight hours.

Why do some hatches appear for an extended period? Some hatches like the Blue Quill just have a long period of emergence, while others like

Spring creeks, such as Virginia's Mossy Creek, have fewer numbers of insect species, but they generally have greater concentrations of hatches. Tricos, Sulphurs, and BWOs are common on spring creeks.

the Little Blue-Winged Olive, Speckle-Winged Dun, Slate Drake, Pink Lady, and Trico have more than one generation each year. And remember, the Little Blue-Winged Olive pattern copies at least a dozen different species of small mayflies.

Sporadic and Concentrated Hatches

To repeat an important aspect of fishing the hatches: Not all hatches are created equal. Some by the manner of their emergence are a much more important source of food than others. Both the dun emergence and the spinnerfall can be sporadic or concentrated. Sporadic hatches and spinner-

Many hatches emerge for an extended period of time, which can be boom or bust for the fly fisher. With hatches like the Trico, trout become highly selective after feeding on it for several weeks.

LENGTH OF HATCHES
(Eastern and Midwestern)

Insect	Pattern Size	Scientific Name	Number of Days*	Time of Year
Black Quill	#14	Leptophlebia cupida	20	April and May
Blue Quill	#18	Paraleptophlebia adoptiva	20	April
Blue Quill	#18	Paraleptophlebia guttata, strigula	120	June, July, August, and September
Blue-Winged Olive Dun	#14	Drunella cornuta	30	May and June
Blue-Winged Olive Dun	#16	Drunella cornutella	30	June and July
Brown Drake	#12	Ephemera simulans	5	May and June
Green Drake	#10	Ephemera guttulata	8	May and June
Hendrickson	#14	Ephemerella subvaria	10	April
Light Cahill	#14	Stenacron interpunctatum	30	May and June
Little Blue-Winged Olive Dun**	#20	Baetis tricaudatus	60	March, April, September, and October
March Brown	#12	Maccaffertium vicarium	20	May and June
Olive Sulphur	#16	Ephemerella needhami	20	June
Pale Evening Dun	#20	Ephemerella dorothea dorothea	40	June and July
Pink Lady**	#14	Epeorus vitreus	29	Late May and again in September
Quill Gordon	#14	Epeorus pleuralis	15***	April, May, and June
Slate Drake**	#12, 14	Isonychia bicolor	40	June and September
Sulphur	#16	Ephemerella invaria	40	May and June
Trico**	#24	Tricorythodes allectus	75	July, August, and September
White Fly	#14	Ephoron leukon	15	August and September
Yellow Drake	#12	Ephemera varia	30	June and July

*Number of days varies from stream to stream and depends to a great extent on weather—this is the number of days a hatch appears on the same stream.
**More than one generation per year.
***Can appear into June on high-elevation streams.

LENGTH OF HATCHES
(Western)

Insect	Pattern Size	Scientific Name	Number of Days the Hatch Appears Each Year on the Same Stream	Time of Year the Hatch Appears	Altitude Where the Hatch Appears
Blue Quill	#18	Paraleptophlebia heteronea	50	June through August	M, H
Blue Quill	#18	Paraleptophlebia memorialis	30	May through July	A
Blue-Winged Olive Dun	#14	Drunella flavilinea	30	Late May through July	M, H
Brown Drake	#10	Ephemera simulans	10	June through July	M
Gray Drake	#12	Siphlonurus occidentalis	30	August through September	A
Gray Fox	#12	Heptagenia solitaria	30	July through September	M, H
Little Blue-Winged Olive Dun	#20	Baetis intercalaris	120	Much of the year	A
Little Blue-Winged Olive Dun	#20	Baetis tricaudatus	120	Much of the year on rivers like the San Juan in New Mexico	A
Pale Evening Dun	#16	Heptagenia elegantula	30	May through July	L, M
Pale Morning Dun	#18	Ephemerella dorothea infrequens	30	May through September	L, M

This chart lists Western hatches and the number of days that they appear. Number of days varies from stream to stream and depends to a great extent on weather—this is the number of days a hatch appears on the same stream. I also include a column for altitude: A (all), L (low), M (medium), and H (high).

			Number of Days the Hatch Appears Each Year on the Same Stream	Time of Year the Hatch Appears	Altitude Where the Hatch Appears
LENGTH OF HATCHES continued (Western)					
Insect	**Pattern Size**	**Scientific Name**			
Pale Morning Dun or Mahogany Dun	#16-18	Ephemerella excrucians	30	May through September	A
Pink Lady	#12	Epeorus albertae	20	June through July	L, M
Quill Gordon	#14	Rhithrogena futilis	30	June and July	L, M
Speckle-Winged Dun	#14-16	Callibaetis spp.	100	April through August	A
Trico	#24	Tricorythodes fictus, minutus	120 (even longer on many southwestern streams)	July through September, in Arizona most of the year	A
Western Green Drake	#12	Drunella grandis grandis	20	Late May through August	L, M
Western March Brown	#14	Rhithrogena morrisoni	80	Late February through April	L

falls don't appear or fall with a thick burst. Concentrated ones do. Sometimes a concentrated hatch or spinnerfall can be too heavy. I can't tell you the number of times I've tried to catch trout rising to a profuse Green Drake hatch. A square foot of water might have a half dozen naturals floating with my fly. What chance does my imitation have to catch a trout? The same goes for the Coffin Fly spinner.

A Coffin Fly spinnerfall occurred one late May evening several years ago. Trout refused the spent spinner pattern, so I purposely tugged the pattern under the surface. In an hour of fishing with that makeshift sunken Coffin Fly, more than a dozen trout hit that makeshift underwater pattern. See chapter 5 on page 70 for more information on that technique.

Which hatch is better to fly-fish over—a concentrated or a sporadic one? If the insect is large, I prefer to fish a sporadic hatch or spinnerfall.

The best hatches to meet and fish are large sporadic ones like the Western Green Drake on the Bitterroot in Montana or the March Brown on the Delaware River in New York. The most frustrating are concentrated ones where your fly has to compete with too many naturals.

> **TIP**
>
> To meet a spectacular hatch, look for one that is *concentrated*; one that *lasts for a long period of the fishing season*; a hatch that is *fairly large* (size 18 hook or larger); and one that usually *rests on the surface* for an extended period.

Small concentrated hatches can be frustrating. Take the Trico spinnerfall on the Missouri River in Montana. So many spinners fell that it was impossible to get trout to take our fly when 10 to 15 naturals floated close by it. The only option available was to use a bouquet that duped trout into believing they were getting several naturals instead of just one. (See chapter 4, page 61.)

Which hatches do you like best? Ideally they should be fairly large; sporadic; ones that lasts for at least an hour, even more; and ones that rest on the surface for some time. These are the variables that make a hatch great and a fishing event memorable.

Top Ten

Your top 10 best hatches might vary tremendously from mine. I base mine on 60 years of fishing the hatches, but one or more of the hatches I list here might not appear on your favorite water. For example, the Brown Drake of the West appears on a restricted number of rivers like Henry's Fork, Silver Creek (both in Idaho), and a few more. That's why it's listed as number 10. The lists are based on overall dependability for the region. With the preceding discussions in mind here they are from the top hatch to the tenth best:

East

1. Sulphur
2. Hendrickson
3. Green Drake
4. Blue Quill (early)
5. Grannom (caddis)

6. Quill Gordon
7. Blue-Winged Olive Dun
8. Little Blue-Winged Olive Dun
9. Trico
10. Brown Drake

Guide Landon Mayer fights a fish on the South Platte River at Spinney Mountain Ranch in Colorado. PMDs, Tricos, and *Baetis* are the major mayfly hatches here.

Midwest

1. Sulphur
2. Hendrickson
3. Brown Drake
4. Michigan Caddis (Hex)
5. Slate Drake
6. Blue-Winged Olive Dun
7. Blue Quill (early)
8. Trico
9. Little Blue-winged Olive Dun
10. Gray Drake

West

1. Pale Morning Dun
2. Western Green Drake
3. Western March Brown
4. Salmonfly (stonefly)
5. *Brachycentrus occidentalis* (Mother's Day caddis)
6. Blue-Winged Olive Dun
7. Little Blue-Winged Olive Dun
8. October Caddis (*Dicosmoecus* spp.)
9. Trico
10. Brown Drake

Pick Your Stream Wisely

A hatch is no better than the stream on which you fish that hatch. And not all streams hold the hatch you want to fish. Some streams hold an inordinate number of fantastic hatches. Anglers often refer to these highly productive streams as insect factories. We all have some favorites where hatches seem to appear almost daily. Two of those "factories" in the West are the Henry's Fork in eastern Idaho and the Metolius River in Oregon. On more than a dozen encounters with those two rivers, I have always encountered hatches. Penns Creek, and to a lesser extent Big Fishing Creek and the Little Juniata River, all in central Pennsylvania, can be

It may sound obvious, but if you want to see great hatches, you must go to streams that have them.

called insect factories. In the Midwest, the Au Sable River in Michigan exhibits the same insect activity. You probably have one or two local streams that produce a varied number of fishable hatches. One thing you've got to constantly remember if you want to match a hatch: Consistently fish a fertile river.

In this section you'll find some of the streams and rivers that hold some specific hatches and a closer look at some of the better hatches. Many of these will also hold angling crowds, so your task is to find some lesser-known waters that hold the same hatch. If you are unfamiliar with area water and have a limited time to fish, then hire a guide.

FISHING HEAVILY FISHED WATERS

The Sulphur hatch was on and Bob Budd and I agreed to meet on a lower section of the Little Juniata River. I arrived at the river at 6:30 p.m. but didn't even get out of the car. Why? At our favorite stretch there were 11 cars parked. I glanced at the river and counted 15 anglers wading in the river near the parking lot. When Bob arrived we decided that we'd head to another nearby stream with a much smaller hatch of Sulphurs. Fishing pressure during the hatches has reached the point of frustration. How did all of this pressure begin?

When I began fly fishing a half century ago, you could go fishing for days and never encounter another fly fisher. To see another fly fisher was indeed the exception and not the rule. But times have changed. Within the past 10 years, fly-fishing pressure on many of our streams has become immense and almost intolerable. And hatches equal crowds. Add a famous hatch to a well-known stream and you're certain to see angling crowds. It's not unusual during a well-known hatch to share a river with hundreds of other fly fishers. I've seen occasions on the San Juan River in New Mexico where guides and anglers have almost come to fisticuffs over fishing territory. What's a person to do?

> **TIP**
>
> Trout on heavily fished waters seem to reject or spit out a pattern more quickly than those on less heavily fished waters.

The decade of the nineties brought a tremendous change to fly fishing. Years ago it was common to catch and kill. Now it is much more common to release that trout so others might enjoy catching it later. The sport grew quickly partly because of the enchantment with the movie *A River Runs*

On highly pressured streams, such as the South Platte, you want to try getting on the water early or staying late to beat the crowds.

Through It. More anglers meant more crowded streams in both the eastern and western United States. More fishing pressure meant more highly selective trout. Fly fishing has changed dramatically in the past 10 years. Ever heavier angling pressure, more sophisticated patterns, and better equipment have arrived on the scene. If older anglers haven't changed, they'll be left behind.

Usually within half an hour of fishing a stream or river—even if I'm the only angler on the stream—I can readily tell if that water gets excessive angling pressure. How? Catch one of the trout and you'll often see a mouth red from getting hooked so many times before. But the way I often determine if a stream is heavily fished is how quickly trout spit out a fly when they strike.

Tony Gehman and Dave Eshenower own Tulpehocken Creek Outfitters in West Lawn near Reading, Pennsylvania. Tony and Dave are both exceptional fly fishers. Several years ago I asked them to take me on a morning trip to see the Trico on the Tulpehocken Creek. We met at a parking lot and waded upstream a half mile to get away from some of the anglers. Wading on this stream in most places is relatively easy, so we headed far enough upstream so we couldn't hear the roar of engines or cars crossing the open iron bridge.

Dave and I decided to fish a three-foot deep riffle while Tony headed to a faster section upstream where he saw some rising trout. Spent female Trico spinners already fell on the surface as we began casting to rising trout. The three of us cast over riser after riser without as much as a refusal. Finally I tied on a sunken Trico Spinner and connected it to the Patriot dry fly in a tandem setup. In the next half hour, I had more than a dozen strikes with that setup but did not manage to catch one trout. We ended the morning landing a dozen trout and missing three times that many. Trout seem to reject flies much quicker on heavily fished waters, and those on the Tulpehocken reflected that hypothesis.

The size of the pattern you use on any heavily fished stream can be important. Dick Henry, a great writer and fly fisher, recently commented about the Trico hatch on the Tulpehocken Creek. He's an acute observer about hatches and how to match them. Here's what he had to say about the Trico hatch on the Tulpehocken:

> Trout that are under heavy fishing pressure can almost become impossible to catch. I remember your writing about [Vince] Marinaro's complaint that the trout in Falling Springs had become annoyingly selective to Trico imitations. Despite a few great days of fishing Tricos below Blue Marsh Dam [on the Tulpehocken] late last season, frustrating times were more common. I remember when netting 15–20 trout a day was reasonably common, but no more. Typically, if they come easy, it comes early in the rise. After that they look and turn away, or if they appear to take the fly they don't get hooked. Ten years ago, I took them easily on a size 22 imitation, but now I'm using 26s and feeling that perhaps my flies aren't small enough.

I agree totally with Dick's observations. When fishing heavily fished waters during a hatch, try offering rising trout a smaller pattern.

Even Canadian trout streams have their crowds. For years I've heard great stories about the Grand River in Ontario and its great trout fishing. Recently Don Bastian and I had a chance to fish the river for a week in early

August. The first morning on the river we experienced a tremendous Trico hatch and spinnerfall. We also experienced something else: From the minute we arrived on the river until we left several hours later, we encountered many other anglers. I caught several trout that morning and all of them had hook marks in their mouths.

The next morning we arrived at the river before 6:00 a.m. so we could beat he crowd. The horde of anglers began arriving about a half hour after we did. By the time Trico spinners fell, I looked up- and downriver and saw more than a dozen other anglers fishing.

There definitely are tactics and strategies that will help you catch trout on heavily fished streams. A fine tippet, the right pattern and size, a drag-free drift, and looking for trout in less-crowded streams and locations on a stream are just a few that work.

SEARCH FOR STREAMS NOT HEAVILY FISHED

Pennsylvania has more than 80 trout streams that hold good Green Drake hatches. Back in 1995 I wrote a book entitled *Mid-Atlantic Trout Streams*

The Henry's Fork is a heavily fished stream, but you can find solitude if you are willing to walk.

Ben Romans, author of *Montana's Best Fly Fishing*, searches the Blackfoot River with a streamer. Ben advises fishing heavily pressured water in the morning, taking a break during the heat of the day, and then returning to the river in the evening for the hatch.

and Their Hatches that included a lot of Pennsylvania and New York trout streams virtually overlooked by many anglers. Many of these streams hold good Green Drake hatches but lack one ingredient often associated with that hatch: angling pressure. It often takes some time to find some of these overlooked gems, but it's well worth it.

I never in my lifetime thought I'd talk about angling pressure in Montana, but I do. At the Bozeman Airport, it was the exception rather than the rule to see someone without a rod case. As I crossed the Madison on my way to the Ruby River I saw dozens of anglers fishing the river. How times had changed in just a couple decades!

FISH EARLY IN THE HATCH
How I look forward to the Sulphur hatch in the East and Midwest each year. The hatch often emerges on the same stream for more than three weeks. I

especially enjoy those first couple of days that the hatch appears. Around the middle of May, the Sulphur often appears for an entire afternoon. At that time trout feed voraciously on these size 16 mayflies. As soon as the hatch begins each year, trout seem eager to strike the natural and the imitation. But after a couple days, the trout grow extremely selective—especially on heavily fished streams. Why does this happen? When the hatch appears and word that the hatch is on get out, throngs of anglers crowd the stream. Look at the Spring Creek as an example of a great trout stream that gets a Sulphur hatch and is heavily fished. Once anglers know that the hatch is on, it's unbelievably difficult to find a good section to fish in solitude. Once the anglers crowd to the stream, the trout get hooked, and soon you'll see bloody mouths, and trout get extremely selective for fear of taking another fake pattern. Often after the hatch is on for a couple of days, trout will drift with the dry fly and inspect it closely. By the end of the hatch, usually three to four weeks later, trout seem to inspect closely every pattern that floats over them before they strike.

What other hatches tend to bring out the anglers? Whether it's Sulphur, Pale Morning Dun, Green Drake, Western Green Drake, or a Trico, try fishing the hatch the first few days it emerges in the season. It usually takes a day or two for the trout to acclimate to a new hatch, but once they do, they feed voraciously on it. If a hatch like the Trico appears for three months, I like to fish it the first week it appears. After the first week you'll often notice a distinct selectivity sets in.

I mentioned earlier that Phil Camera took me to show me the South Platte River and its hatches. Almost from the minute we arrived on that fertile river we saw heavy rainbows feeding within feet of us on Trico emergers, duns, and spinners. Trout fed constantly for the next two hours. But catching these huge rainbows was another story. Evidently these fish saw so many anglers that they fed undisturbed next to us, many times just a few feet away.

> **TIP**
>
> Hatches, especially well-known ones, produce angling crowds. And angling pressure creates wary trout. Look for hatches on less-known streams.

I cast conventional patterns for the first hour and had only one 16-inch rainbow to show for my frustration. Phil had fished the same stretch just a couple of weeks before, when the hatch first appeared for the year, and he had done exceptionally well. But this day, two weeks later, proved to be a frustrating experience.

On some remote Western waters, you can have all the solitude you want. However, keep in mind that solitude does not equal great hatches; in fact, one sign that a river holds great hatches is the amount of pressure it receives.

TOP TRICO WATERS

Ausable River, West Branch, NY
Au Sable River, MI
Battenkill River, VT
Beaverkill River, NY
Big Fishing Creek, PA
Bighorn River, MT
South Platte River, CO
Connecticut River, NH
Deerfield River, MA
Delaware River, NY
Dolores River, CO
Falling Springs Branch, PA
Farmington River, CT
Grand River, Ontario, Canada
Henry's Fork of the Snake River, ID

Housatonic River, CT
Little Lehigh River, PA
Lower Bald Eagle Creek, PA
McKenzie River, OR
Missouri River, MT
North Platte River, WY
Rocky Ford Creek, WA
Ruby River, MT
Salt River, AZ
Silver Creek, ID
South Platte River, CO
Spring Creek, PA
Upper Verde River, AZ
Williamson River, OR
Yellow Breeches Creek, PA

The Trico mayfly group contains four or five common species of the genus *Tricorythodes*. All are very similar and all can create some spectacular surface feeding events, especially on spent spinners. They are diminutive mayflies, ranging from 3 mm (size 24 hook) to 5 mm (size 20). Robert Hall conducted research on Tricos for his doctoral degree at the University of Minnesota. He found several things important to any fly fisher attempting to match this hatch or fall. First, in many areas of the United States the Trico has at least two broods a year. That's why the Tricos last for several months each year. Once the first generation female spinner lays its eggs it takes 49 days for the nymphs to emerge as duns. Second, male duns are of little importance to anglers because they often emerge from 10 p.m. to 2 a.m. Female duns, however, appear in the early morning hours from 6 to 10 a.m. The colder the temperature, the later these duns hatch. So early fall hatches often start after 9 a.m. I've witnessed Trico spinnerfalls in midafternoon in November. Third, members of this genus overwinter as eggs. These eggs hatch out into larvae in May of the following year.

If you fish small hatches—those copied with flies tied on size 20 or smaller hooks—then the prerequisite for a major hatching event is numbers. That's so true with the Trico. If you expect to fish the Trico when lots of trout feed, then you've got to depend on numbers and not size. But one immediate deterrent, especially for the older angler, is the size of the mayfly you're trying to copy. Cheer up! If you are tired of fishing size 24 or 26 flies to match this diminutive hatch, try a bouquet, a fly designed to copy several tied on a size 16 hook. (See chapter 4 on page 60.) Another less-frustrating way to copy this hatch is with a weighted spinner placed below a larger easy-to-see dry fly in a tandem rig.

TOP SULPHUR AND PMD WATERS
PMD

Arkansas River, CO	McKenzie River, OR
Bighorn River, MT	Metolius River, OR
Bitterroot River, MT	Missouri River, MT
Deschutes River, OR	North Platte River, WY
Firehole River, WY	Roaring Fork River, CO
Frying Pan River, CO	Rocky Ford Creek, WA
Green River, UT	San Juan River, NM
Henry's Fork of the Snake River, ID	Silver Creek, ID
Kootenai River, MT	South Platte River, CO
Madison River, MT	Yakima River, WA

Sulphurs

Au Sable River, MI
Beaverkill River, NY
Big Fishing Creek, PA
Cheat River, WV
Deerfield River, MA
Delaware River, NY
Elk Creek, PA
Elk River, WV
Falling Springs Branch, PA
Farmington River, CT
First Fork Sinnemahoning
    Creek, PA

Fishing Creek, PA
Gunpowder Falls River, MD
Holston River, South Fork, TN
Little Juniata River, PA
Lower Bald Eagle Creek, PA
Manistee River, MI
Mossy Creek, VA
Penns Creek, PA
Rose River, PA
Savage River, MD
South Toe River, NC
Spring Creek, PA

The Sulphur (*Ephemerella invaria*) creates one of the first true evening hatches of the season. You can expect to see the Sulphur at 8:30 p.m. sharp. You can almost set your watch on the timing of this hatch. I'll never forget the time I fished Penns Creek with Bob Budd, A.K. Best, John Gierach, and Walt Carpenter. We waited all afternoon for the Sulphur hatch. John Gierach asked me when the hatch would appear, and I told him the duns would emerge at 8:30 p.m. The hatch that evening began at 8:28.

Be prepared for the spinnerfall. On some evenings this takes precedence over the dun. Hatches appear from early May through much of June. Hatches are common throughout the Northeast with one of the heaviest hatches on Spring Creek in central Pennsylvania. Hatches similar to this are found on the Delaware and its tributaries throughout the summer. Maryland's Gunpowder Falls River also holds an excellent hatch of Sulphurs. Hatches of Sulphurs are also found throughout New England in rivers like the Deerfield in Massachusetts and the Farmington River in Connecticut. Streams of the Midwest also hold tremendous hatches. Look for hatches in the Midwest on the Manistee and Au Sable among many others.

Sometimes the Sulphur spinnerfall can rival the importance of the dun emergence. This frustrating situation has happened to me dozens of times. Prepare for both by using a tandem rig. Tie a Sulphur dun as the lead fly and a Sulphur spinner as the point or end fly. That way you have both covered. If the dun is more important, then you can quickly slide on the spinner pattern. If the spinnerfall is more important, leave the dun in place and fish the spinner over sipping trout.

Remember, if you hit the Sulphur hatch the first couple of days that it appears in May, you will often see the hatch begin in the middle of the afternoon and end in early evening. After a day or two of this emergence time, however, the hatch reverts to its normal evening hatching time, 8:30 p.m. That is, unless you hit an inclement day. On those days duns emerge and trout rise all day long.

Pale Morning Duns are the West's answer to the Sulphur. This species (*Ephemerella excrucians*) is found from the Southwest to Alaska. It can produce extremely fishable hatches. The hatch and patterns to match the hatch are eerily similar to the Sulphur. But, the PMD, unlike the Sulphur, can vary in color tremendously. Body colors can range from olive, tan, to pale yellow, so be prepared with several differently colored patterns.

Like the Sulphur, the PMD is significantly affected by bad weather. Add a drizzle, cold weather, or cloudy conditions to a PMD hatch and you will probably experience the hatch of a lifetime.

TOP EASTERN AND WESTERN GREEN DRAKE WATERS
Eastern Green Drake

Beaverkill River, NY	Genegantslet Creek, NY
Big Hunting Creek, MD	Housatonic River, CT
Black Moshannon Creek, PA	Ischua Creek, NY
Cheat River, WV	Kettle Creek, PA
Connecticut River, NH	Little Juniata River, PA
Delaware River, NY	Little Pine Creek, PA
East Koy Creek, NY	Penns Creek, PA
Elk River, WV	Pine Creek, PA
Farmington River, CT	Savage River, MD
First Fork Sinnemahoning	Wiscoy Creek, NY
Creek, PA	Yellow Creek, PA
Fishing Creek, PA	

Western Green Drake

Bitterroot River, MT	Frying Pan River, CO
Black River, AZ	Gibbon River, WY
Colorado River, East Fork, AZ	Hat Creek, CA
Deschutes River, OR	Henry's Fork, ID
Fall River, CA	Kootenai River, MT
Firehole River, WY	Lamar River, WY

Madison River, MT
McKenzie River, OR
Metolius River, OR
Pecos River, NM

Roaring Fork River, CO
Yakima River, WA
Yellowstone River, MT

Many anglers consider the Western Green Drake (*Drunella grandis grandis, D. grandis ingens, D. grandis flavitincta,* and *D. doddsii*) as a super hatch. As hatches go, it has a lot going for it. First, it's huge—a size 12 will copy it. Second, anglers matching this hatch often see these mayflies rest for a while on the surface before taking flight. Third, and best of all for the older angler, these dark slate-olive mayflies appear in the middle of the day. Fourth, the hatch is often sporadic enough that it doesn't totally fill the surface of a stream or river. Trout feed freely on these large duns and fishing the hatch is a delight. The hatch is fairly predictable, and on some waters like the Roaring Fork and Frying Pan rivers in Colorado the hatch moves upriver a couple of miles each day during the emergence season. The hatch begins on the Fork near Glenwood Springs around June 25 and ends at the Ruedi Reservoir on the Frying Pan around Labor Day. That's about 10 weeks of matching this impressive hatch. I first met this hatch below the Ruedi Reservoir back in late August of 1978. When I first saw these huge mayflies appear, I was flabbergasted. Enough emerged that late morning and early afternoon that the huge rainbows in the area fed freely, and they eagerly took the imitation.

The very first time I matched this hatch was more than 40 years ago on the Bitterroot River near Victor, Montana. (See case study #1 on page 38.) But another equally rewarding hatch occurred when Jay Kapolka and I hit the drake on the Metolius in Oregon in late May. Terrible fishing weather made this Oregon trip so spectacular and memorable because many of these large dark duns died on the water. Trout fed on dead and dying duns for more than two hours that day.

Green Drakes (*Ephemera guttulata*) are mainly an Eastern hatch. When I first fished the Minipi River system in Labrador, I eagerly awaited the Green Drake there, but the hatch that appeared, although called the Green Drake by the locals, was instead a large more pale yellow mayfly (*Hexagenia rigida*).

Green Drake hatches occur in enormous proportions. The tales of this huge hatch and the behemoth trout that some anglers who follow this hatch catch are phenomenal.

The late, noted fly-fishing writer Buss Grove habitually followed this hatch from stream to stream. He usually began fishing the hatch on Yellow Creek in southwestern Pennsylvania around May 18 and finished a month or so later on the Beaverkill in New York. In between he fished the drakes on Penns Creek, Big Fishing Creek, and the Delaware River.

I've found more than 80 trout streams across Pennsylvania and New York that hold respectable Green Drake hatches in late May and early June, so the hatch is fairly common. Avoid the crowds fishing that hatch on Penns Creek and Big Fishing Creek in central Pennsylvania, or Yellow Creek in the southwestern part of the state. Look for the hatch on one of the lesser-known waters in the East with less angling pressure. This large mayfly is found on many smaller streams, so don't overlook some of these.

I've often sat back and just watched in awe these huge mayflies emerging on small streams. This large mayfly often has difficulty escaping from its nymphal shuck when emerging. If I get frustrated during this hatch and have trouble catching trout, I add a piece of light tan nylon stocking to the end of the hook—just under the tail of the fly—to imitate a dun with the shuck still attached. (See page 61 in chapter 4.) On some of the smaller streams that hold this hatch, trout often go berserk chasing the duns. It's one of the best opportunities for trout to feed the entire year. Add a shuck the size of the shank of the hook to your pattern that suggests that the fly can't escape rapidly and you're in for some exciting matching-the-hatch fun.

Anglers copy these large mayflies with a size 8 long shank hook, and trout do feed on them. Remember, the size of these mayflies varies considerably, and on smaller waters harboring this hatch a size 10 or 12 long shank fly might more correctly copy the hatch. The two largest trout I ever caught on Green Drake hatches were caught when I purposely tugged the floating dry under the surface. Try that tactic if trout refuse your dry-fly pattern. We discussed this technique in detail in chapter 5 on page 70.

The one thing that continues to amaze me after those four decades of fishing this spectacular, giant hatch is the wide variety of patterns that anglers use. Just take a hike along your favorite Green Drake stream and watch the anglers getting ready for the hatch just prior to its appearance and you'll see what I mean.

Why such a variance in the patterns used for this monster of mayflies? First, the number of fly tiers has increased dramatically in the past couple of decades, and each one feels he or she has the answer to the puzzle. Second, many anglers have experienced success on their own Green Drake pattern.

But the more heavily fished a stream becomes during this hatch, the more selective the trout become.

And there are other challenges. On some occasions, trout seem to take any large, fairly light pattern that they see. But in most instances, when the Green Drake appears so do other hatches like the Sulphur, Slate Drake, Brown Drake, and March Brown. And therein lies the problem: While we insist on fishing a Green Drake pattern, some trout consistently feed on smaller flies like the Sulphur.

The two largest trout I ever caught during the drake hatch were taken on dry flies intentionally dragged under the surface a few inches. This "emerger" often works when nothing else does.

Over the past four decades, I have switched from one Green Drake pattern to another. The one I offer here seems to be the most dependable one for me, especially on heavily fished waters. It's a fairly simplistic, easy-to-tie pattern that has worked on many small, medium, and large waters that harbor the hatch.

Green Drake

Hook:	#8-10 2X long dry fly
Thread:	Cream 6/0
Tail:	Several moose mane fibers
Body:	Cream poly, dubbed and ribbed with the cream tying thread
Wing:	Dark green calftail fibers
Hackle:	One dark brown and one cream hackle

Step 1. Tie in some calftail fibers not quite ⅓ of the way back from the eye of the hook. Don't crowd the eye. Make about 10 wraps with the tying thread in front of the wing to make it stand upright and then divide the wing in two with a series of figure-eight wraps with the tying thread.

Step 2. Take about a half dozen moose mane fibers for the tail and tie them in at the bend. Have the fibers extend past the bend of the hook slightly less than the length of the shank. Cut off the butts.

Step 3. Tie in a piece of the cream tying thread at the bend. Dub some fine poly on to your waxed tying thread.

Step 4. Wind the cream poly up to the wing and then rib the body about five times with the cream tying thread you left behind at the bend. Tie off the body and the ribbing just behind the wing.

Step 5. Tie in the two hackles just behind the wing. Cut off the butts. Make certain the dull side of the hackle is facing forward and wind the two—first behind the wing and then in front of it. I wind more of the brown hackle in the front.

Step 6. Cut off the hackle tips. Cut off the hackle on the bottom so the fly lies flush on the surface.

Step 7. Finish off the head, whip-finish, and apply head cement.

TOP BROWN DRAKE WATERS

Allegheny River, PA	Kettle Creek, PA
Au Sable River, MI	Little Mahoning Creek, PA
Brule River, WI	Manistee River, MI
Cool Spring Creek, PA	Namekagon River, WI
Delaware River, NY	Neshannock Creek, PA
First Fork Sinnemahoning	Pere Marquette River, MI
Creek, PA	Pine Creek, PA
Henry's Fork, ID	Silver Creek, ID
Honey Creek, PA	Skaneateles Lake, NY
Housatonic River, CT	Tionesta Creek, PA
Juniata River, Raystown Branch, PA	

The Brown Drake ranks as one of the most widespread hatches found in the United States. For years many anglers thought this hatch emerged mostly in the West and Midwest. More recently abundant numbers have appeared in many of the northern Pennsylvania streams that flow from north to south like the First Fork of the Sinnemahoning, Sinnemahoning, Kettle, and Big Pine creeks.

But lakes also hold this hatch. Ask Chris Kenney or Bob Foresti about the hatch on Skaneateles Lake just south of Syracuse, New York. They've caught rainbows and smallmouth bass when the hatch appeared in mid-June.

Until recently, anglers searched for this hatch on larger waters like the Delaware and Henry's Fork. But the hatch has been discovered on very small streams like northwestern Pennsylvania's Cool Spring Creek in northwestern Pennsylvania and Honey Creek in central Pennsylvania.

If you hit this hatch, count yourself quite fortunate. The annual hatch is very short-lived and appears on any stream around the end of May in the East, early June in the Midwest, and late June in Idaho. Once the dun emerges, the hatch and spinnerfall occur within a week—often sooner than that.

TOP EASTERN AND WESTERN MARCH BROWN WATERS

Eastern March Brown

Au Sable River, MI
Bald Eagle Creek, PA
Battenkill, VT
Beaverkill River, NY
Big Hunting Creek, MD
Big Pine Creek, PA
Cheat River, WV
Delaware River, NY
Elk River, WV
Farmington River, CT
Genesee River, NY
Housatonic River, CT

Ischua Creek, NY
Little Juniata River, PA
Namekagon River, WI
Penns Creek, PA
Pere Marquette River, MI
Rose River, VA
South Toe River, NC
West Branch of the Ausable
   River, NY
Willowemoc Creek, NY
Wiscoy Creek, NY

Western March Brown

Deschutes River, OR
Henry's Fork, ID
Kootenai River, MT
McKenzie River, OR

Metolius River, OR
Willamette River, OR
Yakima River, OR

Until a few years ago, anglers in the East and Midwest thought they had two mid-May afternoon hatches—the Gray Fox and the March Brown. They matched the Gray Fox with a distinctly lighter pattern. Entomologists have now clumped these two species into one *vicarium* and they have changed the genus, now *Maccaffertium* and not *Stenonema*. I still believe there is a distinct difference between the two; the Gray Fox is decidedly lighter than the March Brown. But I did send one of these light "Gray Foxes" to a highly regarded entomologist, Will Flowers, and he identified the mayfly as a March Brown.

This hatch appears sporadically on the Delaware, Beaverkill, and Willowemoc rivers in New York; the Little Juniata River and Bald Eagle Creek in Pennsylvania; the Deerfield River in Massachusetts; and the Farmington and Housatonic rivers in Connecticut. It usually appears much of the afternoon in sporadic numbers. The beauty of this hatch is captured in the word sporadic. When March Browns appear, they usually do so in very limited numbers, but over a long period of time—sometimes four hours or more. But because the duns are large, they encourage trout to surface-feed even on sporadic duns. On a few occasions, I've witnessed a burst of hatching activity near dusk in mid-May.

The March Brown is a large fly usually copied with a size 12 pattern. The body is ribbed with brown, and that configuration is important when tying a pattern to copy the hatch.

The Western March Brown is a dependable, fairly large mayfly that appears on many far Western waters for more than two months. Look for the hatch to appear from 1 to 3 p.m. from early March through April on waters like the Yakima in Washington and the McKenzie in Oregon. The hatch appears quickly and ends just as abruptly, so be prepared for it. The Western version looks close to its Eastern counterpart but is a bit smaller.

TOP HENDRICKSON WATERS

Allegheny River, PA	Lackawaxen River, PA
Au Sable River, MI	Loyalsock Creek, PA
Beaverkill River, NY	Manistee River, MI
Big Fishing Creek, PA	Namekagon River, WI
Big Pine Creek, PA	Oswayo Creek, PA
Cheat River, WV	Pere Marquette River, MI
Delaware River, NY	Raritan River, South Branch, NJ
Elk River, WV	South Toe River, NC
Gunpowder Falls River, MD	Willowemoc Creek, NY
Housatonic River, CT	Wilson Creek, NC

Anglers eagerly look forward to the Hendrickson hatch (*Ephemerella subvaria*) every spring in the East and Midwest. Show me a good trout stream and I'll show you a good Hendrickson hatch. It is unusual for a stream not to hold this hatch. Dependable hatches are found from I-80 north (a few miles south in some locations) in Pennsylvania. The Delaware River, Willowemoc, and Beaverkill in New York hold outstanding hatches, and the South Branch of the Raritan River in New Jersey has some of these duns in mid-April. In Connecticut look for the hatch on the Housatonic, and in Maryland you'll see the tan to reddish tan bodies of these mayflies on the Gunpowder River. On extremely warm spring days, look for the hatch to appear in the early evening hours.

One problem with the Hendrickson and other early season hatches is that hatches often occur when the water temperature is in the high 40s or low 50s. Often on these days you'll see a spectacular hatch and few if any trout rising to that hatch. A better approach on these cold spring days might be to use a brownish black nymph rather than a dry fly.

Look for the hatch to appear daily from 2 to 4 p.m. for a week or more. Hit a cool overcast day after some warmer weather and you'll be in for a great matching-the-hatch episode. Fish this particular hatch when the early spring weather is inclement; Hendricksons have difficulty taking flight, and you're in for a memorable fishing-the-hatch experience on a drizzly day. On warm spring days it's another matter—Hendricksons then often escape rapidly from the surface—except for the cripples.

Light Hendrickson	
Hook:	#14-16 dry fly
Thread:	Tan 6/0
Tail:	Medium gray hackle fibers
Body:	Tan poly, dubbed
Wings:	Barred wood-duck flank feather fibers
Hackle:	Medium gray

Like the Sulphur you'll find many cripples with this hatch. On the Delaware and Lackawaxen rivers in the Northeast, I've seen hundreds of these dazed and crippled duns unable to take off from the surface.

Probably the best day I've had with the Hendrickson occurred on Oswayo Creek just north of Coudersport in north-central Pennsylvania. On one early spring afternoon thousands of Hendrickson duns appeared— many of them unable to take flight. Many of the duns riding the surface still had shucks attached to them. When this occurs, try a Hendrickson dry with a blackish brown shuck.

Donald Du Bois's seminal book entitled *The Fisherman's Handbook of Trout Flies* gives tying directions for almost 6,000 different fly patterns. That book, written in 1960, is a mainstay in my library, and I refer to it frequently. In that book he lists five separate Light Hendrickson patterns, eight for the Dark Hendrickson, 14 for the Hendrickson, and 10 recipes for the Hendrickson dun. That's a total of 27 fly patterns for Hendrickson flies. Which one is the correct one? The one that catches the most trout on a given day is the correct pattern. Many have a gray tail, gray hackle, and wood-duck barred wings. The major difference in all these patterns is the color and the material used for the body. Most Dark Hendrickson patterns suggest a dark gray body and the Light Hendrickson and Hendrickson a cream, pinkish tan, or tan body.

Why so many patterns for the Hendrickson? Both Du Bois's Hendrickson and Light Hendrickson patterns copy the ubiquitous Hendrickson hatch. The belly of the female natural is tan with reddish or pinkish reflections. The belly of the male is much more reddish, and fly fishers most often copy the latter with a size 14 or 16 Red Quill.

The pattern calls for a body tied with red fox belly fur. You can, however, substitute fine tan poly dubbing. This material is much more buoyant than the fox fur.

Tie up a few of these flies and carry them with you on your early trips. Even if you don't encounter a hatch of Hendricksons, this fly can be an important selection for a memorable day of fly fishing.

TOP BLUE QUILL WATERS

Allegheny River, PA
Au Sable River, MI
Battenkill, VT
Beaverkill River, NY
Big Fishing Creek, PA
Bushkill Creek, PA
Caldwell Creek, PA
Deerfield River, MA
Delaware River, NY
Farmington River, CT
Genesee River, NY
Gunpowder Falls River, MD
Ischua Creek, NY
Little Bald Eagle Creek, PA
North Fork of Moormans River, VA
Rose River, VA
Savage River, MD
White Deer Creek, PA
Wiscoy Creek, VA
Young Womans Creek, PA

The early Blue Quill (*Paraleptophlebia adoptiva*) appears in early to mid April in late morning and early afternoon. The hatch often appears with the Hendrickson, Little Blue-Winged Olive, and Quill Gordon. The Blue Quill is important because it often emerges when weather is miserable or cool and the dun rests on the surface for an extended time. Use a size 18 Blue Quill to copy the hatch. Later Blue Quill hatches (*Paraleptophlebia guttata* and others) that appear in June, July, and August seldom take on the importance of the April one. The hatch is extremely common throughout the Northeast and Midwest.

Hatches can begin appearing as early as 10 a.m. but are most common in the early afternoon hours. Hatches can continue to appear for an hour or two, even more on occasions. The spinner has only minor importance.

TOP BLUE-WINGED OLIVE DUN WATERS
Blue-Winged Olive Dun

Au Sable River, MI	Fishing Creek, PA
Battenkill, VT	Gunpowder Falls River, MD
Beaverkill River, NY	Housatonic River, CT
Brodhead Creek, PA	Kettle Creek, PA
Cheat River, WV	Little Juniata River, PA
Delaware River, NY	Penns Creek, PA
Elk River, WV	Wiscoy Creek, NY

Blue-Winged Flav

Bighorn River, WY	Metolius River, OR
Frying Pan River, CO	South Platte River, CO
Henry's Fork, ID	Yellowstone River, MT
Madison River, MT	

The Blue-Winged Olive dun covers several important mayflies. The first of these to appear is the Blue-Winged *Cornuta* (*Drunella cornuta*), the second is the Blue-winged *Lata* (*Drunella lata*), and the third is the Blue-Winged *Cornutella* (*Drunella cornutella*). Match the *Cornuta* that appear in late May and early June with a size 12 or 14 pattern; and *Cornutella* and *Lata* that appear in late June and early July with a size 14 or 16 pattern.

Heavy and consistent *Cornuta* hatches appear on the Delaware River, the Beaverkill, and Wiscoy Creek in New York; the Little Juniata River in Pennsylvania; the Battenkill in Vermont; and the Housatonic in Connecticut. Look for *Cornutella* hatches on the Little Juniata River, Big Fishing Creek, and Penns Creek in late June.

If you fish any good trout waters in late May and early June, you've probably encountered some heavy hatches of Blue-Winged Olives. Most of these species escape rapidly from the surface—except the cripples and except on lousy days. The Delaware River holds a great early June hatch of these mayflies. I fished this hatch several years back with a Delaware River expert, Bob Sentiwany. Shortly before noon thousands of Blue-Winged

Olives appeared in the early June sun. Just a very few of these mayflies remained on the surface for any period of time. All of the mayflies that rested for an extended period had shucks still attached to their abdomens. I tied on one of my Blue-Winged Olives with a dark Z-lon shuck and cast it toward one of the heavy Delaware River trout rising to the cripples. Again, fish these mayfly hatches on a lousy weather day and you're in for an exciting matching-the-hatch experience.

The Blue-Winged Flav, found on many Western rivers, creates great matching-the-hatch episodes. Look for the hatch to appear in late May on near coastal waters and late June in Rocky Mountain areas. Hatches can appear on the surface in late morning or early evening.

TOP LITTLE BLUE-WINGED OLIVE DUN WATERS

Animas River, CO	Metolius River, OR
Arkansas River, CO	Mossy Creek, VA
Au Sable River, MI	Oak Creek, AZ
Beaverkill River, NY	Penns Creek, PA
Big Fishing Creek, PA	Raritan River, South Branch, NJ
Cache la Poudre River, CO	Red River, NM
Delaware River, NY	Rocky Ford Creek, WA
Falling Springs Branch, PA	Salt River, AZ
Gunpowder Falls River, MD	San Juan River, NM
Henry's Fork, ID	Savage River, MD
South Fork Holston River, TN	Silver Creek, ID
Big Hunting Creek, MD	Spring Creek, PA
Little Juniata River, PA	North Fork of the White River,
Little Pine Creek, PA	MO
McKenzie River, OR	

The Little Blue-Winged Olive can appear almost any time. The pattern and the name copy dozens of small closely related species. One of the most important—*Baetis tricaudatus*—has two generations each year. Match this hatch with a size 18 or 20 Little Blue-Winged Olive in March and April and a size 20 imitation in September and October. Gene Macri has studied this hatch on Falling Springs Branch in south-central Pennsylvania. He found the spring brood of Little Blue-Winged Olives is a size larger than the fall brood.

If you hit a lousy fishing day with drizzle and cool weather during the fishing season, then look for hatches of Little Blue-Winged Olive duns.

You'll find good hatches of Little Blue-Winged Olives on the South Branch of the Raritan River in New Jersey, the Beaverkill, and Delaware rivers in New York; and on Spruce Creek, Spring Creek, the Little Juniata River, Big Fishing Creek, and Falling Springs Branch in Pennsylvania. The Animas in Colorado has a surprisingly good hatch in September. Again, look for heavy hatches in the West on lousy weather days.

But this particular species is only part of the story. There are other Little Blue-Wings almost as important as *B. tricaudatus.* These other closely related species are also copied with a Little Blue-Winged Olive. So carry these patterns in sizes 18 to 22.

TOP SLATE DRAKE WATERS

Ausable River, West Branch, NY	Little Pine Creek, PA
Au Sable River, MI	Little Juniata River, PA
Beaverkill River, NY	Musconetcong Creek, NJ
Connecticut River, NH	Namekagon River, WI
Delaware River, NY	Penns Creek, PA
Esopus Creek, NY	Pere Marquette River, MI
Fishing Creek, PA	Rapidan River, VA
Housatonic River, CT	Raritan River, South Branch, NJ

The Slate Drake appears in late May and June and a second generation in September and October. Even in July and August, however, you'll see occasional duns of this species emerging. Match the spring hatch with a size 10 or 12 pattern and the fall hatch with a size 14 pattern. Slate Drake nymphs often crawl out of the water and on to a rock or other exposed debris to change from nymph to dun. If you plan to fish the nymph, then impart some motion to your imitation to copy this pre-emergence movement. In deep runs, however, these large nymphs change to duns right in the water.

Look for this dark slate gray dun to emerge around 7 p.m. in the spring and late afternoon and early evening in the fall. The Rapidan River in Virginia, Little Juniata River in Pennsylvania, the West Branch of the Ausable River in New York, and the South Branch of the Raritan River in New Jersey hold respectable hatches. In Michigan, the Slate Drake emerges at about the same time that the Hex hatch appears—in June. Check the rocks along fast-water sections to find out if the hatch is under way. If these rocks or other exposed debris hold lots of size 12 black nymphal shucks, be prepared for the hatch that evening.

Anglers call the spinners White Glove Howdys or Maroon Spinners. This phase lands on the surface occasionally, but it is not dependable. The nymphs are excellent swimmers and live freely on the bottom of fairly fast stretches of Eastern and Midwestern waters.

DISTRIBUTION OF SELECTED MAYFLIES

Some mayflies are more widespread than others, such as the ubiquitous Trico. Several Trico species can be found in Canada and just about every state in the lower 48. Anglers can also attest to the commonality of the Pale Morning Dun (*Ephemerella excrucians*). You'll find this mayfly in all of the Western states and as far north as Alaska. And you can fish hatches of Brown Drakes from Idaho to Connecticut. The Green Drake and the Hendrickson, however, are much more limited in distribution, and anglers match hatches of each in a dozen states. If you plan to fish new water or a new area, distribution maps can be extremely important. These maps are just suggestions and some species are found in areas not listed.

Mayfly Quick ID Key

Note: Number at end refers to behavioral characteristics; size is in parentheses (small or large)

EARLY (March 1–May 10)

- **Two tails**
  - *Light*
    - NONE
  - *Dark*
    - *Small*
      - **LITTLE BLUE-WINGED OLIVE DUN (#20)**
        Baetis tricaudatus **and other spp.**
        Olive-gray body with gray wings and tail and tannish gray legs. Dun and spinner move abdomen from side to side when at rest. Species has two generations each year. **Try a** *Baetis* **parachute or emerger.**
    - *Large*
      - **QUILL GORDON (#14)**
        Epeorus pleuralis
        Tannish gray abdomen and legs; gray tails. Emerges on the bottom. Can appear as late as late June, but normally appears the second week in April. **Fish a tannish gray quilled-body wet fly on bottom or a gray-body Compara-dun.**
      - **DARK QUILL GORDON (#14)**
        Ameletus ludens
        Dark gray body, legs, tail, and narrow wings; darker than Quill Gordon. Usually find duns on rocks next to stream. Parthenogenic; you'll find few males. Emerges at the bottom of the stream. **Skitter a gray-body Compara-dun across the surface.**
      - **SPECKLE-WINGED DUN (#14-16)**
        Callibaetis skokianus
        Tan abdomen, legs, and tail with prominent speckled wings. Look for spinners undulating over lakes in late morning. Slow-water or lake species with several generations each year. **Use a tan Compara-dun or thorax pattern; poly spinner.**

169

- **GREAT OLIVE DUN (#12)**
Siphloplecton basale
Olive reflections on a gray body, legs and tail with mottled wings. Of the four large dark early mayflies, this is the least common. Appears around noon in mid-April. **Try a dark olive thorax pattern.**

■ **Three Tails**
  ■ *Light*
  - NONE

  ■ *Dark*
  - *Small*

    - **BLUE QUILL (#18)**
    Paraleptophlebia adoptiva
    Dark brownish gray, thin body. Male spinner undulates over water (flies upward, then drops). Appears from 11 a.m. to 4 p.m. **Try a dark gray parachute pattern or brown-body Compara-dun.**

  - *Large*
    - **HENDRICKSON AND RED QUILL (#14-16)**
    Ephemerella subvaria
    Female has tannish abdomen; male reddish tan. Both have gray wings with medium gray tails and legs. Appears in early afternoon. Since the emerger is important during this hatch, try a **Hendrickson Hair-wing Dun or Snowshoe Emerger.**

    - **BLACK QUILL (#12)**
    Leptophlebia cupida
    Dun has a dark brownish black body, gray wings, dark brown tail and legs. Middle tail of male is shorter than outer two. Active in mid and late April afternoons. **Fish a Black Quill Parachute.**

MIDDLE (May 11–June 30)

■ **Two tails**
  ■ *Light*
  - *Small*
    - NONE

  - *Large*
    - **LIGHT CAHILL (#12-14)**
    Stenacron interpunctatum
    Female is orange-yellow (female spinner has orange-yellow eggs) and male is pale yellow. Both have yellow wings, tail, and legs. Often appears heaviest around 7 p.m. Use a **vernille or thin foam-bodied pale yellow dry fly.**

- **PINK LADY (#12)**

  Epeorus vitreus (female)

  Yellow wings (with olive cast), tail, and legs; abdomen with pink cast. Emerges in early evening. First generation appears in late May and early June and the second in September. **Fish a wet fly deep; try a pink Compara-dun.**

- **LIGHT CAHILL (#14)**

  Epeorus vitreus (male)

  Male's body and wings, legs, and tail are yellow with an olive cast. **Try a yellow Compara-dun.**

- **LIGHT CAHILL (#14)**

  Maccaffertium ithaca

  Has a creamish yellow abdomen, cream legs and wings. Looks lot like *M. vicarium*. **Fish a Parachute Light Cahill.**

- **CREAM CAHILL (#14-16)**

  Maccaffertium modestum

  A very white to cream mayfly dun with cream tails, legs, and wings. Spinner is chalky white. Can be important late in the season. **Try a cream parachute pattern.**

- **MARCH BROWN (GRAY FOX) (#12)**

  Maccaffertium vicarium

  Cream abdomen ribbed with brown. Legs and tail are brown and wings are mottled. Female spinner has orange-yellow eggs and falls to the surface to release them. Appears the last half of May in late morning and afternoon. **Use a cream Compara-dun.**

- ■ *Dark*
  - • *Small*
    - • NONE
  - • *Large*
    - **QUILL GORDON (#14)**

      Epeorus pleuralis

      Tannish gray abdomen and legs; gray wings and tails. Emerges at the bottom of the stream. Can appear in fishable numbers into June, but most hatches usually end by May. **Fish a gray-body Compara-dun.**

    - **DARK GREEN DRAKE (#10)**

      Litobrancha recurvata

      Dark gray with yellow ribbing for the body with gray tail and legs. Has a middle vestigial (just a trace) tail. Large dark gray mayfly (often found on small streams). Usually appears early afternoon. **Use a dark gray Antron emerger.**

- **MICHIGAN CADDIS, GIANT MICHIGAN MAYFLY (#4-6)**
  Hexagenia limbata
  Wings are grayish olive, legs yellow-brown, body yellow on bottom and much darker brown on top, tail is yellowish brown. Giant burrowing mayfly with heaviest populations in the Midwest, but some found as far West as the Williamson River in Oregon. Female spinners release eggs from the air. Female spinner falls to the surface and releases eggs. First appears around the middle of June. Dun appears from 9 p.m. to midnight. **Try a Yellow Paradrake.**

- **GRAY DRAKE (#12-14)**
  Siphlonurus quebecensis, S. mirus
  Male spinner (*S. mirus*) has black rear wing. Dun has brownish black body with gray wings, legs, and tail. Very common in the Midwest. Crawls out of water to emerge on grass, rocks, or logs. **Fish a Gray Wulff with a very dark body.**

- **SPECKLE-WINGED DUN (#14)**
  Callibaetis spp.
  Tan abdomen. Prominent speckled wings. Slow-water or lake species. Look for spinners undulating over lakes in late morning. Has several generations each year. **Use a Callibaetis thorax pattern.**

■ Three Tails
- *Light*
  - *Small*
    - **PALE EVENING DUN (#18)**
      Ephemerella dorothea dorothea
      Body, legs, and tail are pale yellow and wings are a very pale gray. Appears at dusk a couple weeks later than the Sulphur. **Try either a Quick Trim fly or a vernille or foam-bodied Sulphur.**

  - *Large*
    - **GOLDEN DRAKE (#12)**
      Anthopotamus distinctus
      Yellow to pale orange-yellow body, wings, tail, legs. Weak veins in the wing. Appears the third week in June. **Fish a Golden Drake Paradrake.**

    - **SULPHUR (#14-16)**
      Ephemerella invaria
      Pale yellow body with olive cast, cream legs, and tail, and pale gray wings. Female spinner has orange-yellow eggs. Most often appears at 8:30 p.m. Often appears as a cripple. Begins in the East near mid-May. **Use a Quick Trim fly or a vernille or foam-bodied parachute Sulphur.**

- **PALE EVENING DUN (#14-16)**
Penelomax septentrionalis
Male has bright red eyes; body, tail, and legs are yellow and wings are pale gray. **Try a vernille-bodied Sulphur dun.**

- **YELLOW DRAKE (#12)**
Ephemera varia
Body, legs, and wings are yellow with the wings, legs, and tail banded darker. Last of the three large drakes (*Ephemera* spp.) to appear. Appears most commonly at 8:45 p.m. **Fish either a pale yellow Compara-dun or Quick Trim fly.**

■ *Dark*
  ● *Small*
    - **BLUE QUILL (#18)**
Paraleptophlebia mollis, P. guttata
Dun's body, tail, and wings are slate-gray to dark brown. Legs are tannish cream. Male spinner is called the Jenny Spinner and has a hyaline or white body with a few hind segments dark brown. Male spinner undulates over water (flies upward, then drops). **Fish a dark gray parachute pattern.**

    - **DARK BLUE QUILL (#16)**
Teloganopsis deficiens
Body is dark gray, almost black with dark gray wings and tail; darker than the Blue Quill. Appears at evening in early June (around 7 p.m.). **Use a Black Gnat Parachute.**

    - **LITTLE BLUE-WINGED OLIVE DUN (#20)**
Danella simplex
Gray wings and pale gray legs with an olive body. **Choose a *Baetis* Parachute or a *Baetis* emerger.**

    - **OLIVE SULPHUR (#16)**
Ephemerella needhami
Female has olive body; male dark brown. Legs, tail, and wings are cream on the female. The male has a cream tail and legs and dark slate wings. **Use an olive vernille-bodied parachute for the female dun, and a dark brown Compara-dun for the male.**

    - **CHOCOLATE DUN (#16-18)**
Eurylophella bicolor
Legs are cream; chocolate-brown body with a dark gray tail. **Fish a chocolate Compara-dun.**

- *Large*

  - **GREEN DRAKE (#8-10)**

    Ephemera guttulata

    Body is cream (dark on top and cream on bottom), wings heavily mottled with green and gray reflections. Front legs dark brown, rear two pairs cream. Tail is dark gray and legs are mixture of green, yellow, and dark brown. Large mayfly varies in size tremendously. Male spinners undulate among the trees waiting for females. Has a two-year life cycle. Trout often prefers feeding on emerger patterns. Appears in late May or early June. **Use a cream Compara-dun, Drake emerger, or Spent Deer Hair Coffin Fly.**

  - **BROWN DRAKE (#10-12)**

    Ephemera simulans

    Dun has grayish tan body and wings with dark brown tail and legs. Spinner is darker gray brown. Male spinner undulates over water (flies upward, then drops) and undulates among the trees waiting for females. Emerges in the East near the end of May; in the Midwest in early June, and in the West in late June. **Try either a dark brown Compara-dun or emerger pattern.**

  - **BLUE-WINGED OLIVE DUN (#14)**

    Drunella cornuta

    Has a medium olive body with gray-olive tail, creamish gray legs, and dark gray wings. Emergers work well because dun takes off rapidly, except in the most inclement of conditions. Hatch often has cripples and rides low in the water. Heaviest appearance is late May and early June. **Choose an olive emerger, Blue-Winged Olive thorax, parachute, or Antron spent-wing dark olive spinner.**

  - **BLUE-WINGED OLIVE DUN (#16)**

    Drunella cornutella

    Dun has a medium olive body, gray wings, and tannish olive tail and legs. Female spinner has dark olive eggs. Not as common as *cornuta* or *lata*. Appears in early to mid June. **Use an Antron spent-wing dark olive spinner or Blue-Winged Olive thorax pattern.**

  - **BLUE-WINGED OLIVE DUN (#16)**

    Drunella lata

    Another olive-bodied mayfly with olive-gray tail and gray wings that appears three weeks later than *D. cornutella*. Female spinner has dark olive eggs. Spinnerfalls can be tremendously important. **Fish an Antron spent-wing dark olive spinner or Blue-Winged Olive Thorax pattern.**

- **SLATE DRAKE (#12-14)**
  Isonychia bicolor
  Front legs are dark brown; rear two pairs are cream. Body, tail, and wings are dark slate gray. Female spinner falls to the surface and releases eggs, which are olive-brown. Emerges often out of the water on grass, rocks, or logs, so fish nymphs toward shore. First generation appears in late May and June (#10-12) and the second in September and October (#14). **Try a black Angora nymph or dark Gray Wulff.**

LATE (JULY 1–OCTOBER 30)

■ **Two tails**
- *Light*
  - *Small*
    - **NONE**
  - *Large*
    - **CREAM CAHILL (#14-16)**
      Maccaffertium modestum
      Dun has a cream body, legs, wings, and tail. One of the lightest mayflies other than the *Ephoron* species. Often found late in the season. **Try a cream Compara-dun.**

    - **WHITE FLY (#14)**
      Ephoron leukon
      Tail and wings are a pale gray, body is cream-white, front legs are dark brown, and rear ones are cream. Legs atrophied except for forelegs of male. Try dragging your dun pattern. **Fish a White Wulff.**

- *Dark*
  - *Small*
    - **LITTLE BLUE-WINGED OLIVE DUN (#20)**
      Baetis tricaudatus, B. intercalaris, or *Plauditus veteris*
      Olive-gray body with gray wings and tail and tannish gray legs. *P. veteris* is more olive than others. Dun moves its abdomen from side to side while at rest. **Choose a *Baetis* parachute or emerger pattern.**

  - *Large*
    - **BIG SLATE DRAKE (#8)**
      Hexagenia atrocaudata
      Body, legs, tail, and wings are dark tannish gray. Two-year life cycle. Female spinners release eggs from the air. Male spinners undulate about 30 feet in the air around 7 p.m. in early August. **Use a tannish gray Paradrake.**

■ Three Tails
■ *Light*
• *Small*

• TRICO
Tricorythodes allectus (#24)

Female dun has a pale cream-green body with cream legs and tail and pale gray wings. Female spinner has white rear abdomen, dark brown front part of abdomen, and thorax with dun tails and cream legs. Male has a dark brown body, legs, and tail. The male spinner body is ribbed finely with white. Glassy, clear wings. Female spinner has dark olive eggs. Females fall first and males last. One of few male spinners to consistently fall on the water's surface. Species has two or more generations each year. **Choose a White and dark brown (female) or dark brown (male) spent-wing poly Trico spinner with a few strands of Krystal Flash in the wings.**

• LITTLE WHITE MAYFLY (#24-26)
Caenis **spp.**

A white very small mayfly with a brown thorax, pale gray wings, and tannish white legs and tail. **Try a Color Matcher fly.**

• *Large*

• WHITE FLY (#14)
Ephoron leukon

An almost totally white fly that emerges and dies within an hour or two. Female—all legs atrophied (not fully developed). Female spinner falls to the surface and releases eggs. If a drag-free float doesn't work, try dragging the fly a foot or two in front of a riser. **Use a White Wulff or pale gray nymph.**

• YELLOW DRAKE (#12)
Ephemera varia

Wings, legs, and body are mottled yellow and dark brown. Tail is darker. Hatches aren't as heavy as Brown and Green Drakes. Female spinner falls to the surface and releases eggs. Appears most commonly at 8:45 p.m. **Fish a yellow Quick Trim fly.**

■ *Dark*
• *Small*

• TRICO (#24)
Tricorythodes allectus

Female: Pale cream-green body with cream legs and tail and pale gray wings. Male has a dark brown body, legs, and tail. The body is ribbed finely with white. Female spinner has dark olive eggs. Male spinners form an elongated ball and female spinners enter the swarm. One of few male spinners to consistently fall on the water's surface. Species has two or more generations each year. **Fish a spent-wing poly spinner in either white and dark brown or dark brown (male). Add a few strands of Krystal Flash to the spent wings; add a few strands of smolt-blue Krystal Flash to the poly wings.**

- **BLUE QUILL (#18)**
  Paraleptophlebia guttata
  Wings are medium gray; body and tail are slate-gray; and legs are tan. A midsummer to fall hatch that anglers confuse with Tricos. Appears for weeks and weeks from June to October. **Use a gray-bodied or brown-bodied Compara-dun to match this morning hatch.**

- *Large*

  - **YELLOW DRAKE (#10)**
    Ephemera varia
    Back is darker than the creamish yellow abdomen. Hatches aren't as heavy as Brown and Green Drakes. Appears most commonly at 8:45 p.m. **Choose a yellow-brown Compara-nymph or Quick Trim fly.**

  - **SLATE DRAKE (#14)**
    Isonychia bicolor
    Front legs are dark brown; rear two pairs are cream. Body, tail, and wings are dark slate-gray. Female spinner falls to the surface and releases eggs, which are olive-brown. First generation appears in late May and June (#12) and the second in September and October (#14). Emerges often out of the water on grass, rocks, or logs, so fish nymphs toward shore. **Try a Black Angora nymph or dark Gray Wulff.**

WESTERN

EARLY (MARCH 1–MAY 10)

■ **Two tails**
  ■ *Light*

    - **NONE**

  ■ *Dark*

    - *Small*

      - **LITTLE BLUE-WINGED OLIVE DUN (#20)**
        Baetis tricaudatus, B. intercalaris
        Olive-gray body with gray wings and tail and tannish gray legs. Dun and spinner move abdomen from side to side. (Note: Appears again in the fall.) **Fish a *Baetis* Parachute or a *Baetis* emerger.**

    - *Large*

      - **WESTERN MARCH BROWN (#14)**
        Rhithrogena morrisoni
        Overall looks like the eastern March Brown with a tannish belly, mottled tannish yellow legs, wings, and tail. Appears for more than three months on some Western rivers. Begins in late February on near coastal and coastal trout waters. Can be smaller than #14. **Use a brown Compara-dun.**

- **SPECKLE-WINGED DUN (#14)**
  Callibaetis **spp.**
  Body and legs are grayish tan, and wings are dark gray. Prominent speckled wing. Found on lakes and ponds and very slow water of streams. Several generations each year. Some generations can be smaller than #14. **Fish a CDC *Callibaetis* Compara-dun.**

■ **Three Tails**
  ■ *Light*
  - NONE

  ■ *Dark*
  - *Small*
    - **BLUE QUILL OR MAHOGANY DUN (#18)**
      Paraleptophlebia memorialis, P. heteronea
      Dark brown body; tail and wings are slate-gray. Legs are tannish cream. Male spinner undulates over water (flies upward, then drops). **Use a gray-bodied or brown-bodied Compara-dun to match this morning hatch.**

    - **TRICO (#24)**
      Tricorythodes explicatus, T. fictus
      Pale creamish green body with cream legs and tail and pale gray wings. Female spinner has white rear abdomen, dark brown front part of abdomen and thorax with dun tails and cream legs. Male has a dark brown body, legs, and tail. The male spinner body is ribbed finely with white. Glassy, clear wings. Female spinner has dark olive eggs. *T. fictus* can be larger. Females fall first and males last. Male spinners form an elongated ball and female spinners enter the swarm. One of few male spinners to consistently fall on the water's surface. Emerges as early as February in the Southwest. **Fish a spent-wing poly Trico spinner in either white and dark brown or dark brown (male). Add a few strands of Krystal Flash to the spent wings.**

  - *Large*
    - NONE

MIDDLE (May 11–July 15)

■ **Two tails**
  ■ *Light*
  - *Small*
    - NONE

- *Large*
  - LIGHT CAHILL (#12)

    Cinygma dimicki

    Creamish yellow body with cream legs marked darker. Tail is tan and wings are tannish cream. Appears in Montana in late June and early July. **Use a pale yellow Compara-dun.**

  - PINK LADY (#12)

    Epeorus albertae

    Wing are gray with cream-gray with pinkish cast on female body; tail is creamish tan and legs are cream with darker markings. Emerges at the bottom on the stream. Appears in the evening. **Use a pale yellow Compara-dun for the male and a pink Compara-dun for the female.**

  - PALE BROWN DUN (#14)

    Rhithrogena hageni

    Body is tannish olive, wings are gray, and legs and tail are cream. Typical fast-water species. Emerges in early July in Montana. **Fish a brown Parachute.**

  - PALE EVENING DUN (#14)

    Heptagenia elegantula

    Has a cream body, legs, and tail and gray wings. **Use a yellow Compara-dun.**

- **Dark**
  - *Small*
    - DARK BROWN DUN (#20)

      Diphetor hageni

      Dun has dark gray wings, dark brown body; legs and tail are tannish cream. Heavy on Henry's Fork in Idaho. Emerges in the afternoon in late June and early July. **Fish a small dark brown Parachute.**

    - LITTLE BLUE-WINGED OLIVE DUN (#20)

      Baetis bicaudatus

      More olive body than *B. tricaudatus* with olive legs and tail and gray wings. Emerges in the afternoon in early July. **Try a *Baetis* emerger or *Baetis* Parachute.**

  - *Large*
    - SPECKLE-WINGED DUN (#14)

      Callibaetis spp.

      Body and legs are grayish tan, and wings are dark gray with typical speckled venation. Prominent speckled wing. Found on lakes and ponds and very slow water of streams. Several generations each year; can be smaller. **Fish a *Callibaetis* thorax when the dun appears.**

- **QUILL GORDON (#12)**
Rhithrogena futilis, R. undulata
R. futilis has a tannish gray body, legs, and tail with medium gray wings. *R. undulata* has a reddish brown body with a gray tail and wings and brown legs. Appears in the morning and afternoon. **Try a tan Parachute.**

- **GRAY DRAKE (#12)**
Siphlonurus occidentalis
Body is brownish black ribbed lighter with gray tail and grayish tan legs. Wings are brownish gray with distinct venation. Female spinner has green eggs. Emerges often out of the water on grass, rocks, or logs. Appears in the afternoon usually in July. **Fish a Gray Wulff.**

■ **Three Tails**
  ■ *Light*
    ● *Small*

- **PALE MORNING DUN (#18)**
Ephemerella dorothea infrequens
A small mayfly with creamish yellow body, legs, and tail and pale gray wings. **Fish a small yellow Sparkle Dun.**

- **PALE MORNING DUN (#16)**
Ephemerella excrucians
Body color of this mayfly varies considerably from stream to stream. Body color can be tan, pale olive, cream-yellow, or reddish tan. Most often the body is creamish yellow with an olive cast with pale gray wings and creamish yellow tail and legs. **Fish a small Sparkle Dun or PMD.**

- **TRICO (#20-24)**
Tricorythodes explicatus, T. fictus
Pale cream-green body with cream legs and tail and pale gray wings. Female spinner has white rear abdomen, dark brown front part of abdomen, and dark brown thorax with dun tails and cream legs. Female spinner has dark olive eggs. Male has a dark brown body, legs, and tail. The male spinner body is ribbed finely with white. Glassy, clear wings. *T. fictus* is a bit larger and is found mainly in the Southwest. Male spinners form an elongated ball and female spinners enter the swarm. Females fall first and males last. One of few male spinners to consistently fall on the water's surface. **Fish a spent-wing poly Trico spinner in either white and dark brown or dark brown (male). Add a few strands of Krystal Flash to the spent wings.**

- *Large*
  - NONE
- **Dark**
  - *Small*
    - TRICO (#20-24)

      Tricorythodes explicatus, T. fictus

      Female spinner has dark olive eggs. Male emerges from 10 p.m. to 2 a.m. They land on vegetation and don't become active until daylight. Depending on the temperature they become active spinners around 8 a.m. Female duns now emerge, change to mating spinners within minutes. Males form a ball or swarm and females enter this swarm, mate, drop out of the swarm, then move to the water and lay their fertilized eggs. Females fall on to the surface first, followed by a combination of females and males, then mostly males fall. The latter species, *T. fictus,* is a bit larger and is found mainly in the Southwest. One of few male spinners to consistently fall on the water's surface. **Fish a spent-wing poly Trico spinner in either white and dark brown or dark brown (male). Add a few strands of Krystal Flash to the spent wings.**

    - DARK BLUE QUILL OR MAHOGANY DUN (#18)

      Paraleptophlebia vaciva, P. debilis

      Dark brown body; tail and wings are slate-gray. Legs are tannish cream. Male spinner undulates over water (flies upward, then drops). Emerges in midsummer but may appear later. **Use a dark brown thorax to match the dun.**

  - *Large*
    - BROWN DRAKE (#10)

      Ephemera simulans

      Grayish tan body and wings with dark brown tail and legs. Found across the United States. Male spinner undulates over water (flies upward, then drops). Male spinners undulate among the trees waiting for females. Emerges in the East near the end of May, in the Midwest in early June, and in the West in late June. **Fish a dark brown Compara-dun or use a dark brown emerger.**

    - WESTERN GREEN DRAKE (#10-12)

      Drunella grandis grandis

      Body is grayish black with olive reflections and ribbed with pale yellow. Legs are grayish black with pale tips. Wing is dark grayish black and tail is dark brown with a pale gray tip. Several important subspecies. Large dark olive-gray mayfly found on the surface in late June in the Rockies and late May on near coastal waters. **Use a lifelike Green Drake Paradrake for the hatch.**

- **BLUE-WINGED OLIVE DUN (#14-16)**
Drunella flavilinea
Body is medium olive with grayish olive tails, and creamish olive legs and gray wings. Appears in the morning and evening. **Choose a Blue-Winged Olive thorax fly to copy the hatch.**

LATE (July 15–September 30)

- Two tails
  - *Light*
    - *Small*
      - NONE
    - *Large*
      - **GRAY FOX (#14)**
      Heptagenia solitaria
      Pale gray wings with a yellow cast and a body of yellowish tan; legs and tail are tannish gray. Found on the Colorado River in Colorado around 7 p.m. in late August and early September. **Fish a yellow Parachute.**

      - **PALE EVENING DUN (#16)**
      Heptagenia elegantula
      Cream body, legs, and tail, and gray wings. **Use a yellow Compara-dun.**
  - *Dark*
    - *Small*
      - **DARK BROWN DUN (#20)**
      Diphetor hageni
      Dun has dark gray wings, dark brown body; legs and tail are tannish cream. Heavy on Henry's Fork in Idaho. Appears in the afternoon in late June and early July. **Fish a small Dark Brown Dun Parachute.**

      - **LITTLE BLUE-WINGED OLIVE DUN (#20-22)**
      Baetis bicaudatus, B.tricaudatus
      B. tricaudatus has olive-gray body with gray wings and tail and tannish gray legs. *B. bicaudatus* has a more olive body than *B. tricaudatus*. Dun and spinner move abdomen from side to side. Second generation might be a bit smaller than the spring one. **Try a *Baetis* emerger or *Baetis* Parachute for a dry fly.**

- *Large*

  - **GRAY DRAKE (#12)**

    Siphlonurus occidentalis

    Body is brownish black ribbed lighter with gray tail and grayish tan legs. Wings are brownish gray with distinct venation. Appears in afternoon. **Use a Gray Wulff when the hatch appears.**

  - **SPECKLE-WINGED DUN (#14)**

    Callibaetis **spp.**

    Body and legs are grayish tan, and wings are dark gray with typical speckled venation. Prominent speckled wing. Found on lakes and ponds and very slow water of streams. Emerges often out of the water on grass, rocks, or logs. Several generations each year. **Fish a** *Callibaetis* **thorax when the dun appears.**

■ Three Tails
  ■ *Light*
  - *Small*

    - **PALE MORNING DUN (#16)**

      Ephemerella excrucians

      Body color of this mayfly varies considerably from stream to stream. Can be tan, olive, pale yellow, reddish tan. Body color can be tan, pale olive, cream-yellow, or reddish tan. Most often the body is creamish yellow with an olive cast with pale gray wings and creamish yellow tail and legs. Hatch can occur almost any time of day or evening. **Choose a small Sparkle Dun or PMD when the dun hatches.**

    - **TRICO (#20-24)**

      Tricorythodes explicatus, T. fictus

      Pale cream-green body with cream legs and tail and pale gray wings. Female spinner has dark olive eggs. Male spinners form an elongated ball and female spinners enter the swarm. *T. fictus* is a bit larger and found more in the Southwest. One of few male spinners to consistently fall on the water's surface. Some hatches appear year-round in the Arizona and New Mexico areas. **Fish a spent-wing poly spinner in either white and dark brown (female) or dark brown (male). Add a few strands of Krystal Flash to the spent wings.**

  - *Large*

    - **WHITE FLY (#14)**

      Ephoron album

      Pale gray tail and wings with legs in which front are dark and rear ones white; body is white with grayish cast. All legs atrophied except for front legs of male. Male has two tails and female has three. **A White Wulff works well during the hatch.**

- *Dark*
  - *Small*
    - DARK BLUE QUILL OR MAHOGANY DUN (#18)

      Paraleptophlebia vaciva, P. bicornuta

      P. vaciva dun's body, tail, and wings are dark grayish brown. Legs are tannish cream. *P. bicornuta* is a darker gray. Male spinner undulates over water (flies upward, then drops). *P. vaciva* emerges in midsummer; *P. bicornuta* usually in September. **Use a gray-bodied or brown-bodied Compara-dun to match this morning hatch.**
  - *Large*
    - NONE

Down-Wing Quick ID Key

- *Light*
  - *Small*
    - NONE
  - *Large*
    - LIGHT STONEFLY (#12)
      Isoperla signata
      Belly is pale yellow; tail and legs are light tan. Emerges in early May in the afternoon. **Fish a yellow Stimulator.**

    - CREAM CADDISFLY (#14)
      Psilotreta spp.
      Cream belly and darker legs and wings. Appears above water the first week in May. **Try a cream Parachute Caddis.**

- *Dark*
  - *Small*
    - LITTLE BLACK STONEFLY (#18)
      Capnia vernalis
      Body, legs, and wings are almost totally black. Can emerge as early as January, most often in February; late morning and afternoon. **Fish a black Elk Hair Caddis.**

  - *Large*
    - EARLY BROWN STONEFLY (#12-14)
      Strophopteryx fasciata
      Body and legs are brown with tannish wings. Early April afternoons. **Use a brown Elk Hair Caddis.**

    - LITTLE BLACK CADDIS (#16 OR 18)
      Chimarrha aterrima
      Body is black with dark wings and dark brown legs. Appears in early and mid April. **The Orange Caddis Larva created by Ben Rooke works well in a stream holding plenty of these caddisflies.**

- **GRANNOM (#12-16)**
  Brachycentrus **spp.**
  Color of the body is from greenish brown to black with dark gray wings and darkish brown legs. Common in the East in mid-April. **Use a green or black Elk Hair Caddis.**

- **GREEN CADDIS (#14)**
  Rhyacophila lobifera
  Body is olive-green, wings are mottled brown, and legs are tannish brown. Appears in early May. **Fish a green Elk Hair Caddis.**

MIDDLE (May 11–June 30)

- **■ Light**
  - **● Small**
    - **NONE**
  - **● Large**
    - **LITTLE GREEN STONEFLY (#16)**
      Alloperla imbecilla
      Lime-green body with pale green wings and legs. June mornings and afternoons. **Choose a green Stimulator pattern.**

    - **LITTLE YELLOW STONEFLY (#14-16)**
      Isoperla bilineata
      Yellow stonefly called the Yellow Sally by anglers with a yellow body, pale yellow wings, and yellow and tan legs. Appears in June. **Try the yellow Stimulator to copy the hatch.**

    - **TAN CADDIS (#16)**
      Symphitopsyche slossanae
      Wings are mottled brown with a tan body and legs. **Try Walt's Worm to copy the larva or a Deep Sparkle Pupa to copy the emerger.**

- **■ Dark**
  - **● Small**
    - **NONE**
  - **● Large**
    - **GIANT STONEFLY (#8)**
      Pteronarcys dorsata
      Clear gray wings with short black tails and black legs, body with orange markings. The largest common stonefly in the East. Appears above water in late May and early June in the evening. **Use a pattern like the black Stimulator for this giant stonefly.**

- **GOLDEN STONEFLY (#10)**
  Acroneuria abnormis
  Body is golden yellow; tail and leg are dark brown. Late May and June. **Fish a golden Stimulator.**

- **DARK BLUE SEDGE (#14)**
  Psilotreta frontalis
  Dark gray body; gray wings and legs. **Try fishing a dark gray-bodied Elk Hair Caddis when this hatch appears.**

LATE (July 1–October 30)

- *Small*
  - **NONE**
- *Large*
  - **OCTOBER CADDIS (#8-10)**
    Pycnopsyche spp.
    Has a ginger-amber belly with yellow wings and legs. Species can rest on the surface for some time, making it an important down-wing to match. Often appears on warm evenings in late October. **Use an orange Stimulator.**

WESTERN
EARLY (March 1–May 10)

- ■ *Light*
  - *Small*
    - **NONE**
  - *Large*
    - **OLIVE STONEFLY (#12)**
      Suwallia pallidula
      Dark olive body with darker tails and legs. Often appears before snowmelt begins. Emerges in early May in the afternoon. **Fish an olive Elk Hair Caddis.**
    - **CREAM CADDISFLY (#14)**
      Psilotreta spp.
      Cream belly and darker legs and wings. Appears above water the first week in May. **Fish a Cream Parachute caddis.**

- *Dark*
  - *Small*

    LITTLE BLACK STONEFLY (#14-18)

    Capnia vernalis

    Body, legs, and wings are almost totally black. Can emerge as early as January, most often in February; late morning and afternoon. **Fish a black Elk Hair Caddis.**

  - *Large*

    - **EARLY BROWN STONEFLY (#14)**

      Strophopteryx occidentalis, S. fasciata

      Body and legs are brown with tannish wings. *S. fasciata* is active around noon in April. **Try a brown Stimulator.**

    - **LITTLE BLACK CADDIS (#16)**

      Chimarrha aterrima

      Body is black with dark wings and dark brown legs; larva is bright orange. Appears in early and mid April. **An orange wet fly should work at this time of the year; try an Orange Caddis Larva created by Ben Rooke in a stream holding plenty of these caddisflies.**

    - **GRANNOM (#12-16)**

      Brachycentrus spp.

      Color of the body is from greenish brown to black with dark gray wings and darkish brown legs. Often called the Mother's Day Hatch; appears in April and May. **Try a green or black Elk Hair Caddis.**

    - **GREEN CADDIS (#14)**

      Rhyacophila lobifera

      Body is olive-green, wings are mottled brown, and legs tannish brown. Appears in early May. **Try a green Elk Hair Caddis.**

MIDDLE (May 11–June 30)

- *Light*
  - *Small*

    - **NONE**

  - *Large*

    - **LITTLE OLIVE STONEFLY (#14)**

      Alloperla imbecilla

      Lime-green body with pale green wings and legs. Appears afternoons in June. **Try an olive Stimulator.**

- TAN CADDIS (#16)

  Symphitopsyche **spp.**

  Body is tan and legs and wings are darker. **Try Walt's Worm to copy the larva and and Deep Sparkle Pupa to copy the emerger.**

- LITTLE SISTER SEDGE (#14-16)

  Cheumatopsyche campyla

  Body is dark brown as are the tail and legs. Mornings and afternoons in late June and early July. **Fish a brown Elk Hair Caddis.**

- LITTLE YELLOW STONEFLY (#14-16)

  Isoperla **spp.**

  Pale yellow body with tan legs. Appears in June. **Try the yellow Stimulator to copy the hatch.**

- GOLDEN STONEFLY (#6)

  Calineuria californica

  Body is golden with dark brown tail and legs. Pale wings lie flat on body. **Use a golden Stimulator.**

■ *Dark*

  ● *Small*

    - NONE

  ● *Large*

    - GREEN SEDGE (#14)

      Rhyacophila lobifera

      Olive-green body with tan legs and light mottled brown wings. Appears in the East in early May. **Fish a green Elk Hair Caddis.**

    - MOTHER'S DAY CADDIS, GRANNOM (#14)

      Brachycentrus occidentalis

      Body ranges in color from green to black with dark brown legs and wings. **Use a green or black Elk Hair Caddis.**

    - SALMONFLY (#8)

      Pteronarcys californica

      Natural has an orange body and dark brown legs, tail, and antennae. The largest common stonefly in the West. Appears above water in late May and early June on the Deschutes in Oregon and as late as early July on the Yellowstone River. **Use an improved Sofa Pillow or Simple Salmon to copy this important stonefly. Nick Nicklas created the latter pattern, which is highly productive. It's like five small caddisflies tied on one large long shank hook. Use a Grindle Nymph to copy the larva.**

- **GOLDEN STONEFLY (#8)**
  Calineuria californica
  Body is golden yellow with dark brown tail and legs. A large stonefly found in late May and June. **Use a golden Stimulator.**

LATE (July 1–October 30)

- *Light*
  - *Small*
    - NONE
  - *Large*
    - NONE
- *Dark*
  - *Small*
    - NONE
  - *Large*
    - **SALMONFLY (#8)**
      Pteronarcys californica
      Natural has an orange body and dark brown legs, tail, and antennae. The largest common stonefly in the West. Appears above water in late May and early June on the Deschutes in Oregon and as late as early July on the Yellowstone River. **Use an improved Sofa Pillow or Simple Salmon to copy this important stonefly. Nick Nicklas created the latter pattern, which is highly productive. It's like five small caddisflies tied on a large long shank hook orange body. Use a Grindle Nymph to copy the larva.**

    - **WILLOW FLY (#8)**
      Skwala americana
      Dark brown bodies with legs and tail the same general color. A Western hatch. **Use a brown Stimulator.**

    - **OCTOBER CADDIS (#6-10)**
      Dicosmoecus spp.
      Has an amber to orange-colored belly with amber brown legs and tan wings. Species can rest on the surface for some time, making it an important down-wing to match. The McKenzie River in Oregon has a great hatch. Often appears in October. **An orange Stimulator works well during the hatch.**

Index